THE DRUDGE REVOLUTION

THE
DRUDGE
REVOLUTION

The Untold Story of How Talk Radio, Fox News, and a Gift Shop Clerk with an Internet Connection Took Down the Mainstream Media

MATTHEW LYSIAK

BenBella Books, Inc.
Dallas, Texas

BenBella Books, Inc.
10440 N. Central Expressway, Suite 800
Dallas, TX 75231
www.benbellabooks.com
Send feedback to feedback@benbellabooks.com

BenBella is a federally registered trademark.

Printed in the United States of America
10 9 8 7 6 5 4 3 2 1

Library of Congress Control Number: 2019055523
ISBN 9781948836968 (print)
ISBN 9781950665150 (ebook)

Editing by Joe Rhatigan
Copyediting by Miki Alexandra Caputo
Proofreading by Sarah Vostok and Ashley Casteel
Indexing by Debra Bowman
Text design and composition by PerfecType, Nashville, TN
Cover design by Ty Nowicki
Cover image © iStock / gerenme
Printed by Lake Book Manufacturing

Distributed to the trade by Two Rivers Distribution, an Ingram brand
www.tworiversdistribution.com

Special discounts for bulk sales are available. Please contact bulkorders@benbellabooks.com.

To Hilde Kate Lysiak

CONTENTS

PART 2

A NOTE ABOUT SOURCES

This book is the summation of 192 personal interviews and hundreds of newspaper articles and court documents.

Matt Drudge did not agree to be interviewed for this book, but whenever possible I used Matt's own words from speeches, interviews, and his book, *Drudge Manifesto*.

I have honored the request of a select handful of interview subjects who asked that I protect their identity for fear of retribution.

Every statement of fact is from either a direct source from a published account or court document.

Joseph Curl, the only employee ever employed full-time by the Drudge Report, has agreed to tell his story for the first time because he's afraid much of the story will be lost. He told me, "There's so much misinformation out there about Doc [Matt Drudge], and I feel like someone needs to set the record straight."

PROLOGUE

The Debate

The team of senior advisers for Donald Trump, the Republican nominee for president, were deep in the bowels of the University of Nevada, Las Vegas, Thomas & Mack Center, minutes away from the third debate on October 19, 2016, when a phone rang.

It was Matt Drudge. He was in the building and someone needed to get him to Trump right away.

Trump's son-in-law, Jared Kushner, advisers Kellyanne Conway, Reince Priebus, Chris Christie, Rudy Giuliani, Corey Lewandowski, David Bossie, and Steve Bannon all looked at each other, dumbfounded.

"Where is he?" one of them asked.

"He's in the audience," another answered.

———

As sole proprietor of the Drudge Report, Matt Drudge has been labeled everything from the Walter Cronkite of his era to a "dangerous menace" and the "country's reigning mischief-maker." However, no one disputes Matt's influence. A single link from his website has the power to move news cycles, shape front pages, rush television producers into a desperate scramble, and send tremors all the way to 1600 Pennsylvania Avenue.

The site has become the de facto talking points for the right-leaning media. Its archaic black letters can be seen over Rush Limbaugh's shoulder on his Dittocam, and regional conservative talk radio hosts from across the country openly admit to taking their cues for what to talk about from his site.

According to Jonathan Martin and Ben Smith from Politico, Matt has the "ability to drive the national conversation with what he chooses to highlight on his site." Republican media consultant Alex Castellanos has claimed that Drudge has become Centre Court at Wimbledon. "If it doesn't happen there, it doesn't happen." Investigative journalist Carl Bernstein called Drudge "an influence unequaled in American politics."

The *Hill*'s Brent Budowsky wrote, "Far more than any individual in the media, Drudge dominates his competitors to the degree that he has no competitors, and determines what you watch on television, what you read in newspapers, what you hear on radio, and even what you read on the internet about politics more than any single person in American history."

For more than two decades, Republican communication strategy has officially relied on leaking items to the Drudge Report. By 2007 the Democratic Party had a small staff that was responsible for trying to influence the publisher of the Drudge Report.

Matt Drudge, who had barely squeaked by with a high school education, has been credited for everything from the impeachment of President Bill Clinton to the death of print news.

But on the night of October 19, 2016, one of the most powerful men in the history of media was sitting discreetly in the Las Vegas auditorium, unnoticed by the thousands of people in the crowd.

Just the way he liked it.

For those who had accompanied the Republican nominee to the debate, the sense of anticipation came with the full knowledge that the moments to follow in the debate would forever change the trajectory of each one of their lives. Perhaps no one understood that more than Steve Bannon, who had left his position as executive chairman of Breitbart.com when he was appointed chief executive of Donald Trump's presidential campaign. A Trump defeat would very likely relegate Bannon to a footnote in history, but a victory would vault him into one of the most consequential positions of power in the world. And Bannon knew it. He also understood that the chances of a Trump victory appeared to be more rooted in fantasy than political reality. RealClearPolitics polling showed Democratic nominee Hillary Clinton with a seemingly insurmountable seven-point lead.

Still, the campaign wasn't without hope. Internal polling showed a much tighter race with hopes resting on the belief that non-college-educated white voters were being underrepresented in major national polls.

Donald Trump was minutes away from going onstage. His advisers needed to pull Matt out of the audience right away for a quick one-on-one with their candidate, but there was a slight problem: Did anyone even know what Matt Drudge looked like?

Over the past decade, Matt had disappeared from the public eye. He openly brags that it's been years since anyone has managed to snap his picture. If someone does pull out a phone in his presence, Matt covers his face with his hands.

His mysterious persona was consciously cultivated in the belief that the Drudge Report would be more powerful without a public face attached to it. "Let the Drudge Report be," he told a friend before going dark. "Remove the face. Remove the target. Just let the Drudge Report stand for itself." And Matt's instincts would be proved right.

By October 2016 the site's power had reached new levels. Only weeks earlier, during a radio interview, Texas senator Ted Cruz placed the blame for his electoral defeat on Matt Drudge. And Cruz wasn't alone. Jared Kushner, who had forged a relationship with Matt months earlier, knew from his time as publisher of the *New York*

Observer that the support of the Drudge Report was crucial to his father-in-law's electoral chances.

But with only minutes to go until Trump hit the stage for what was expected to be one of the most consequential debates in American political history, a senior staffer asked, "Is there anyone who can pick him out of the crowd?"

David Bossie spoke up. "I know what he looks like."

Bossie had met Matt several times in the late 1990s. The two had formed a mutually beneficial relationship over common enemies—Bill and Hillary Clinton. Bossie raced through the underground labyrinth of tunnels beneath the stadium until he emerged through an opening facing the audience. He scanned the crowd. Several rows up he spotted an unshaven man in his early fifties wearing dark glasses and a brown fedora.

It was Matt Drudge.

PART
1

1

DELIVERY

When the bell rang on the afternoon of March 31, 1981, many of the students at Montgomery Blair High School in Silver Spring, Maryland, headed to the local movie theater, the Silver, to catch the third installment in the Omen series or piled into cars for a cruise down Carroll Avenue with REO Speedwagon's *Hi Infidelity* blaring through the tape deck.

But for one fourteen-year-old, all the action was happening on a wooden park bench. There, under the shade of a tall eastern hemlock, the young man, pencil in hand, raced through the pages of the local newspaper, the *Washington Star*.

The broadsheet's headline that day would be a variation of the same one running in the nearly seven thousand newspapers across the country: PRESIDENT SHOT! It had been less than twenty-four hours since the assassination attempt on Ronald Reagan, and the news was still raw.

Reporters on the ground in Washington, DC, were scrambling to find pay phones. From there, they would relay the bits and pieces of information back to television producers in New York City, where it would then be projected onto teleprompters or relayed into the ear-pieces of network anchors before streaming out to the American public.

The first reports were that President Reagan was unharmed. A member of the Secret Service had been shot, but the president had been removed to a secure location. A gunman had been identified: twenty-five-year-old John Warnock Hinckley Jr. of Evergreen, Colorado.

Then came another report, this one claiming that President Reagan *had* been shot. A bullet had punctured the president's chest, but he had suffered no vital damage.

Meanwhile, a very different narrative was unfolding out of public view: the president had collapsed in the emergency room and was near death. Communication with Vice President George H. W. Bush, who was traveling by air at the time, was spotty, as was the question of who was in charge of running the United States of America.

But the biggest question of all hanging over those who had been hastily assembled in the Situation Room in the basement of the White House was whether this assassination attempt was a Soviet plot that was going to thrust the nation into World War III.

All these subplots would remain hidden from the American public, but not for a lack of good reporting. A handful of well-sourced journalists had been made aware of both President Reagan's condition and the suspicions of a Soviet-inspired attack. The information had been fed up the news chain, but somewhere along the way the decision had been made to keep it from the public.

But it was the large, bold, black words scrolled across the top of the *Washington Star* that enthralled the young man on the park bench. He knew he could do better if he was in charge. He began making slashes through the dark print.

The lede is buried in graf eight.
Slash.

As soon as his pencil finished marking up one story, it moved on to the next one.

This page 2 story should be on page 12.
Slash.

He was an artist. The bench, his office. The pencil, his tool. The newspaper, his canvas.

This isn't even a news story.
Slash.

His position may have been at the very bottom of the media food chain—newspaper carrier in the *Washington Star*'s circulation department—but Matt Drudge had no interest in job titles. He was exactly where he wanted to be—working his first job in media.

"On the bench I would play editor," he would later write. "I'd rewrite my own headlines for an audience of one."

"I noticed how *their* lead story was not really *the* lead story. How the hottest news was buried on the inside pages and the best reporting was riding at the end of the copy when it should have been at the beginning."

Not only was the pay more than sufficient to meet the young man's needs, but the job had another, more important perk: owning the delivery route meant he would be first in his neighborhood to know the news. "I was never sure why I cared about being first, but boy did I feel connected when I was," he would remember.

———

Matthew Nathan Drudge was born on October 28, 1966, the only child of two liberal Democrats, Robert and Deborah Drudge.

They had married two years earlier in Chicago, Illinois, before making the move to Maryland to begin their new family. The young couple decided to plant their middle-class roots in what is now the Takoma Park Historic District. Deborah's mother signed for a mortgage for them to purchase a bungalow-style home on New York Avenue. Robert Drudge paid the mortgage with his $30,000-a-year job as a psychologist for the Department of Human Resources with the state of Maryland. Meanwhile, Deborah was completing her education in hopes of becoming a lawyer. In June 1973 she passed the bar. From all outward appearances, the young family seemed destined to thrive.

As both parents worked their way up the rungs of the socioeconomic ladder, Matt grew up a latchkey kid. He was a contemplative child who was naturally drawn to meditation. Radio was an early passion for young Matt, and at night he narrated his own personal radio shows into a tape recorder before falling asleep to the talk radio voices crackling through the AM stations on his transistor radio.

Despite growing up with two parents both immersed in liberal politics, Matt was largely apolitical. He had a fondness for both Jimmy Carter and Ronald Reagan and immersed himself in pop culture, spending afternoons sitting in front of the television watching his favorite soap opera, *The Young and the Restless*. And he always loved newspapers, especially poring over the insider political maneuvering chronicled by the *Star*'s liberal columnist Mary McGrory.

With a healthy mix of older retirees, families, and young professionals willing to commute the seven miles to Washington, DC, the upper-middle-class neighborhood of Takoma Park proved an ideal place for the young boy brimming with energy.

"I remember climbing trees and rolling down hills and raking leaves and throwing acorns and sliming fireflies on the sidewalk and watching them glow," Matt would later remember. "I'd stare at the clouds and daydream. I had my own little world."

"I grew up in a typical American family."

———

But the tall, lanky kid with ears that seemed to outpace the growth of the rest of his body was anything but typical. When Matt was six, his father moved out of the house. He had met another woman, and they moved in together on a soybean farm in Tyaskin, Maryland, where Robert took care of his new girlfriend's two sons. A few months later, on October 15, 1975, Robert officially divorced Deborah.

The divorce and child-support papers in the Maryland State Archives offer a heart-wrenching picture of a desperate mother struggling to raise a troubled son. Deborah was awarded custody, and Robert was required to pay $200 a month, an amount Deborah claimed wasn't nearly enough. Robert got a second job as a family counselor with the Catholic Social Services, earning an extra $50 a week. On the weekends he made pocket change as a musician and became heavily involved in his church, where he began preaching. On September 25, 1977, he gave a sermon at the Salisbury Unitarian Fellowship on the topic of "Societal Regression." "Religion Is Man's Understanding of the Universe and His Place in It," the teaser in the local newspaper read.

Deborah got a job as a staff attorney in the office of Senator Edward Kennedy, working as a liaison between the private sector and the government on health-related issues. Deborah described this position as "more of a public relations/government relations lobbyist type job than strictly a lawyer."

Matt would later describe his mother proudly as a "pioneering lawyer"; however, her career stalled just a few years after passing the bar. Following the divorce, Deborah Drudge fell ill, and in January 1980 she was forced to leave her job owing to "severe illness."

She became a patient of Dr. Norman E. Rosenthal, who would later become prominent for having been the first to describe seasonal affective disorder and for pioneering the use of light therapy. Dr. Rosenthal prescribed a "radical new treatment" for Deborah that appeared to worsen her condition.

Her sickness soon became debilitating. She told the court in her plea for more child support, "I'm still going through a convalescence and they hope that I'll be back to work soon, but it's sort of open-ended at this point."

Deborah changed her last name from Drudge to Star and her first name from Deborah to her middle name, Claire. Unable to support herself, Claire had to lean on her mother to help with the mortgage. She sold her Datsun 280Z.

Meanwhile, the family turmoil had predictably trickled down to Matt. In September 1980 he began his freshman year at Montgomery Blair High School, where he struggled.

"I was bored with it all," Matt wrote of his time in school. "It was rigid, it was stupid, it was a lot like the news coverage now. There's very little originality going on. Everything I've learned I've learned on my own. I'm self-taught. I've kept some original thinking or what I think is original."

Matt was also forgetful. He lost his eyeglasses. He lost his books. He was suspended a few times for cheating on tests and liked to brag that his only extracurricular activities were passing notes and cutting classes. His mother attributed his poor grades to "special education" needs. The school recognized him as a "student on the fringe."

Matt remembered this time differently. "I stopped learning at age twelve," he later recalled. "They were not able to stuff me like a sausage. Even then I didn't play by society's rules. I was a rebel all the way."

For enjoyment, Matt listened to the police scanner. In the summer, his mother sent him to camp. Claire recalled her son enjoyed movies and video arcades. Music became another passion for Matt. His mom bought him records, a stereo, a Walkman, and cassette tapes.

———

Court papers reveal that the young man's issues extended far beyond a rebellious attitude. Matt had been dealing with "emotional problems" since the divorce.

"Physically he's in good shape, but emotionally he has problems and he's getting treatment for that," Claire told the court. On June 18, 1981, Matt was arrested for making "annoying phone calls." He was taken to Montgomery County Juvenile Court, where his issues were blamed on his father, who resented him for being "disturbed." Coupled with his mother's health troubles, it was suggested Claire send Matt to a foster home.

The agonizing situation was described to the court by a relative testifying in support of Claire:

> After he went to his diagnosis well he got is a problem of making annoying phone calls to a girl, so that's what precipitated the testing, and as a result of the testing the diagnosis was that the boy was disturbed. Not that he has a mental illness but because of his life situation of his mother's sickness and his father resents him that he is disturbed and needs treatment, and their recommendation was a boarding school if we could afford it or possibly a foster home if one could be found, that is one of the reasons we are here is for more money to hopefully send him through boarding school and if not the last choice will be a foster home.

2

THE BIG THREE

I n the early '80s, the American media landscape was dominated by
the network newscasts and a burgeoning print newspaper market.

Newspaper circulation was on an upward trajectory that would
continue for the next eight years, with many big-city publications
putting out multiple editions per day. The influence of print spread
to the network newscasts, with headlines from that morning's *New
York Times*, *Chicago Tribune*, and other prominent dailies often used
as crib sheets for the producers at ABC, NBC, and CBS, and would
later feature as the lead stories for the nightly newscasts. And the Big
Three were enjoying a wave of success of their own, riding a formula
of viewer trust and familiarity. But a cloud of uncertainty was also
hovering forebodingly over this balance of power.

At ABC News, station president Roone Arledge was busy reboot-
ing *ABC World News Tonight* and was determined to jump-start the

⸗ast out of its perennial third-place finish, having chosen Frank ∩olds to occupy the anchor chair after Harry Reasoner and Bar-ιra Walters left in 1978.

NBC's *Nightly News*, which had a strong grip on second place in the evening news ratings war for most of the '70s, was now betting on the success of John Chancellor to help catapult the network to number one. Audiences were already familiar with Chancellor, who, along with David Brinkley and Frank McGee, had worked as one of three anchors who rotated in a coanchor format in the early '70s.

But it was the retirement of Walter Cronkite at *CBS Evening News* that sent shock waves through the country. For nineteen years, audiences had made a habit of turning the dial to hear directly from "the most trusted man in America." It was Cronkite's criticism of America's role in the Vietnam War that was instrumental in President Lyndon Johnson's decision not to seek reelection. Reportedly, Johnson, who was watching Cronkite's broadcast live in the White House, turned to aides and said, "If I've lost Cronkite, I've lost Middle America." CBS News correspondent Dan Rather, who had risen to prominence by sassing President Richard Nixon, had been named as Cronkite's successor.

For ABC and NBC, Cronkite's exit was an opportunity to finally knock the ratings goliath off its pedestal. But there was another uncertainty looming on the horizon. For decades, the Big Three had a tight-fisted monopoly on the television news medium, but all that was about to change.

Newcomer Ted Turner's twenty-four-hour news station CNN had launched on June 1, 1980.

Meanwhile, across the ocean, Australian newspaper tycoon Rupert Murdoch was spreading his media empire, having just put in bids to purchase the *Times* and the *Sunday Times* newspapers in the UK, all the while closely watching the experiment unfolding at CNN.

In 1980 talk radio was still mired in a holding pattern, hindered by the Federal Communications Commission's postwar fairness doctrine of 1949, which allowed the government control over how controversial issues were to be discussed, forcing the holders of broadcast licenses to spend airtime appeasing the commissioners.

The rule made debating controversial ideas unprofitable, but the recent election of a conservative administration promised a reevaluation of the rule.

In Sacramento, California, few took note when a little-known disc jockey named Rush Limbaugh made the decision to leave radio entirely to accept a position as director of promotions for the Kansas City Royals.

The new decade also delivered exciting new advances in technology.

In San Francisco, a 1981 KRON newscast told the story of a radical experiment happening at the *San Francisco Examiner* that had the potential to revolutionize how the public gathered news.

"Imagine, if you will, sitting down to your morning coffee and turning on your home computer to read the day's newspaper," the newscast began. The story continues with a print newspaper subscriber named Richard Halloran, identified by the segment as a "home computer owner." By placing a simple phone call, Halloran was able to access most of the newspaper without stepping foot outside his front door. "When the telephone connection between these two terminals is made, the newest form of electronic journalism lights up Mr. Halloran's television with just about everything the *Examiner* prints in its regular edition—that is, with the exception of pictures, ads, and the comics."

Eight newspapers, including the *New York Times*, the *Los Angeles Times*, and the *Washington Post*, had already joined the computer network, with more joining every week.

his is an experiment," said *Examiner* editor David Cole. "We are
ıg to figure out what this will mean to us as editors and reporters
ıd what it means to the home user . . . And we are not in it to make
money. We are probably not going to lose a lot but we are probably
not going to make much either."

The segment concluded with KRON newscaster Steve Newman
presciently saying, "Engineers now predict the day will come when
we get all our newspapers and magazines by home computer, but
that's a few years off."

3

NORTHWOOD

After struggling through his freshman year at Montgomery Blair High School, the decision was made to have Matt transferred to Northwood High School for his sophomore year. It would mean a longer commute—forty-five minutes one way—but Claire hoped it would provide her son with a fresh start.

On his first day at his new school, Matt wore a fedora with an index card tucked inside its band. On the card Matt had scrawled the word "Press."

The strange hat was more than a fashion statement or an ode to his love of journalism. Northwood High classmate Joël Glenn Brenner remembers, "He always had that hat on. And it never came off. He played with it when he was bored or lowered it down to use it as a shield when he wanted you to leave him alone."

ssmates weren't sure what to make of him. He dressed differ-
ie acted different. Even his voice was different.

"The thing about Matt that most people will find very hard to
elieve is that the person people know with the hat and with the whole
shtick, that was never an act. That was always him. It was the way
he acted when nobody paid any attention," says Brenner. "He didn't
create some persona. That's just Drudge being Drudge," she adds.

His aloof personality was on display in the classroom. Matt never
felt the need to pretend to be engaged in his education. He came to
school holding a copy of the *New York Times* tucked under his arm.

Brenner remembers, "It was strange because no one in that
school even read the *New York Times*. If the teacher was talking and
he wasn't interested, Matt just leaned back in his chair, pulled his
paper out, and began reading. He was a real maverick. A lot of people
thought he was a nut."

Matt was always reading. If it wasn't a newspaper, he read books
by libertarian authors Robert A. Heinlein or Ayn Rand. Matt would
walk down the hallway toting a large hardcover copy of Rand's mag-
num opus *Atlas Shrugged*, which gave a blueprint of her philosophy
of individualism and rational self-interest that she called objectivism.

But more than the strange hat or the newspapers and books, it
was Matt's attitude that stuck out to his peers. For instance, when
Matt and his classmates were instructed to make videos introducing themselves for speech class, Matt chose instead to share his philosophy on life. In the video, he sat behind a desk, slouched over
while presenting his libertarian view of the universe. As one student
recalled, "[This] was before anyone in the school really knew what
libertarianism was. It was brilliant, but so different that I don't think
the teacher knew what to do with it. [Matt] failed the assignment. The
teacher said to Matt, 'That was great but it wasn't the assignment,
and what's with the accent?' But Matt just shrugged. He didn't care.
That was who he was."

To most of the guys, Matt seemed like a total wacko, but to the theater geeks and English types, he was cool because he was his own person. Brenner recalls, "I remember being a little bit awestruck that someone could be so out there on their own island and be okay with it because Northwood was very much about fitting in."

Matt didn't participate in extracurricular activities. He didn't do his homework or go to football games or homecoming dances. He also didn't join the school newspaper, but a few fellow students recall him reading the morning announcements broadcast over the school loudspeaker, including leading the Pledge of Allegiance. He said stuff to raise eyebrows and be provocative so that he could watch how teachers and other students reacted.

Brenner reflects,

> Matt was the kind of guy who always liked to be in the know and he let you know he was in the know. He spoke up and participated and always had his own point of view, which was usually way out there from whatever everyone else was thinking. Matt always acted like he knew more than anybody. He listened to his own drummer. Always. I admired him for it because it was not cool how he acted, but you could tell that Matt legitimately did not give a shit.

"People just didn't know what to make of him and he liked it that way. He liked to keep people guessing," she adds.

If Matt did embrace an identity during his Northwood years, it was counterculture, remembers classmate Beth Eriksson. Eriksson had become friends with Matt during his sophomore year when both were exploring the early '80s DC club scene.

"Most of us at Northwood were a very, very tight-knit group of people. Matt was extremely reclusive. Almost withdrawn from his remembers Eriksson. "Matt and I were both on the fringe of school society. We didn't really do anything mainstream. He was ᵢnitely punk, but more on the new-wave punk side."

Beth and Matt would go to the Wisconsin Avenue punk shop Commander Salamander, and then at night they hit the clubs in Georgetown or the legendary F Street concert venue Nightclub 9:30 in Washington, DC, to hear punk music. "He was very confident, really cocky, snooty kind of guy. He definitely came across like he was better than the rest of us. He was goofy and odd and sometimes annoying," she adds.

Matt's nasally voice and odd behavior made him a target of the football players.

In one instance, Matt was hanging out at a local park when someone shouted a gay slur. Matt picked up a rock and hurled it toward the boy, missing badly. The young man returned fire. The rock smashed Matt in the face, resulting in stitches.

A former classmate remembers, "Most of the kids were pretty mean to him, if they noticed him at all. He took it all in, but it was his decision to not fit in. He stayed away from most people. Never partied. He made a serious decision to not fit in and so teachers looked at him as a problem child."

Rosalind Flynn, who taught drama and public speaking at Northwood, remembers Matt as a talented, bright student who had a natural proclivity toward theater. Matt took Flynn's advanced acting class as a senior, and she remembers that he was a good actor. "He had great comic timing. A dry delivery of lines. We cast him in a sketch as Superman, and Matt was great."

Flynn's class would put together small productions and invite other classes to come. Once onstage Matt shined and appeared to enjoy the attention it brought. But Matt was still a difficult student. He refused to apply himself or bend to the rules of the school, no matter the consequences.

"I recognized Matt as a great public speaker, but if he didn't like the criteria that was set up for the speech he just wouldn't do it. He would say, 'Nope, not doing it that way,'" says Flynn. In other instances, Matt would have weeks to prepare, but would instead deliver an impromptu speech he had made up in his head minutes before his presentation was due. Flynn tried to talk to him. He was always very nice and respectful, but he refused to engage himself in her classroom.

And it wasn't just the lack of effort that vexed Flynn. Matt had figured out a way to manipulate Northwood High School's grading system. Montgomery County had a grading policy where each semester grade was calculated on a trend. "Matt had figured out that if he got an A in the first quarter, he could do zero work in the second quarter, and I couldn't fail him. As soon as the second quarter began, he came to class and did nothing," says Flynn.

Flynn tried her best to convince the administration to change the policy, but since it seemed to be working for all the other students, they left the policy in place, and Flynn couldn't fail Matt. "He was very shrewd. At the time, I was very annoyed, but at the same time, I couldn't help but admire him," adds Flynn.

In the beginning of his junior year, Matt met a quiet sophomore named Michelle Brooks. The connection was instantaneous.

"Matt had spent a lot of time alone, and so did I. And we were both kids coming from broken families, and we just clicked," Michelle remembers.

Michelle would tease Matt about his tendency to overapply his Chaps cologne. Matt came back at her with a tongue-in-cheek nickname—Mrs. Thing.

The two also bonded over their shared love of music and dreams of escaping Maryland. They talked a lot about their futures. How one day they were going to move away from Silver Spring to a more glamorous location like Paris, New York City, or California.

Matt found another advantage in becoming friends with Michelle: she had access to one of his favorite papers, the *Unicorn Times*. Michelle volunteered as a proofreader at the free alternative paper, which billed itself as "Washington's most complete entertainment calendar since 1973" and a one-stop coverage for music reviews, performer profiles, and most important, as far as Matt was concerned, the emerging new-wave and punk scenes.

While easily found in the metro areas, in the rural areas where Matt and Michelle lived copies of the *Unicorn Times* had become a much-sought-after commodity. Michelle earned Matt's favor by hooking him up with copies as soon as they came off the press. It wasn't long after meeting that the two began spending nearly every day together.

Michelle forged notes to get Matt out of school, and they would take the Metro into the city, where they spent hours exploring. On Friday afternoons they would go to Little Tavern to buy a bag of burgers and then hit the Value Village thrift store to sift through the discount racks.

"Matt would always buy his old-man hats and dress shirts that were two sizes too large for his frame. Big jackets. New wave-ish. And these large, old-man shoes that were always too big for him," says Michelle.

Meanwhile, at school, Matt seemed unfazed by the attention his wardrobe drew. "He was really loud and would say ridiculous things. He would try to draw attention to himself. People laughed at him a lot. When I was with Matt, they made more fun of me than normal. At first, I was kind of embarrassed, but soon I got used to it. It was like Matt and I were in our own worlds," says Michelle.

———

After school the two usually ended up at Matt's. His house was striking for its lack of personality and warmth. "There were no pictures on the wall. There were a few pieces of furniture, but no throw pillows on the couch or anything extra. Just the bare essentials," Michelle recalls. Matt explained that his mom just hadn't felt compelled to brighten the house up, telling Michelle that his mother was sad.

Matt's mom was rarely home, but when she was, Michelle could tell that something was off. Michelle remembers Claire as a small-ish, attractive woman with long brown hair parted down the middle, who looked like a hippie but without "that warm, easygoing hippie vibe." There was something different about the cadence of her voice and the look in her eye. "She didn't seem all there. She seemed to be struggling with something very serious." When Michelle asked what was wrong, Matt just shrugged his shoulders, explaining that she was "still upset about the divorce."

The other thing Michelle noticed was Matt's strained relation-ship with Claire. "Matt didn't like his mom," says Michelle. "He talked down to her. He would sometimes just look at her and say dismis-sively, 'That's my mother.'"

Unlike the rest of the house, Matt's bedroom was brimming with personality. There were black sheets on Matt's bed and a pur-ple disco ball blaring colors across the white walls. When the door closed behind them, the duo blasted Frankie Goes to Hollywood or the English electronic jazz-funk band Freeez and danced on his bed.

———

On top of not feeling connected to his mom, Matt rarely saw his dad. "Except for me, Matt was a loner," says Michelle.

Every night Matt wrote his thoughts down on paper, and then shared them with Michelle the next day on the bus to school. Some-times the notes were four to five pages long. He wrote about the world and how superficial people were as well as how much he hated high school and how one day he was going to take Michelle to Paris. Other times the notes included handwritten lyrics from his favorite songs. In one instance, Matt wrote out the words to "IOU" by Freeez.

Do you realize some things you say
I know you do, it makes me so confused
I'm sure this ain't the way that love should be
Let's get it right, it's much too good to lose.

As the relationship evolved, Matt began to use the notes to open up about his sexuality and his relationships with men. It hardly came as a revelation to Michelle.

"Most of the school thought of Matt as gay, so I wasn't surprised at all. It was really no big deal to me," says Michelle. "He was just so out there and never dated any girls, and the way he behaved and the things he would talk about . . . People just weren't like that back then, especially in a football-oriented school like Northwood."

While unfazed by Matt's sexuality, Michelle was taken aback by how explicit the notes were in describing the details of his intimate relationships. On the bus rides home from school at the end of the day, Matt demanded that Michelle give him his notes back so he could destroy them.

———

Matt never dated classmates, but by the age of eighteen had already made himself a staple at the Washington, DC, gay club scene. Matt knew all the doormen, and even though Michelle wasn't yet of age, he could get her in without a problem.

By the mid-1980s DC had a flourishing gay community. Beginning in the 1970s, clubs catering to alternative lifestyles started taking over the strip along 9th and 14th Streets NW, taking advantage of cheaper rents. Club Washington, a gay bathhouse, opened in the early 1970s, followed by the strip club Heat and the drag bar and strip club complex Ziegfeld's/Secrets.

Matt's favorite clubs were located in Dupont Circle. Michelle preferred to go to Nightclub 9:30, a straight club. On some nights, the two would make a deal. If Matt went with her to 9:30, she would then agree to go to the gay clubs with Matt.

At the clubs, Matt met men from all across the country. "Matt always dated older men," Michelle remembers. "I remember him going down to North Carolina to meet with some man in his fifties. Even though he was still in high school, Matt would fly or take Amtrak to various destinations around the country and even Canada one time. Every year he would travel somewhere. He never told me how he paid to get there, but I always assumed the other person he was meeting was paying."

Matt never drank or did recreational drugs at the clubs, but his dancing was epic. "Matt would dance the whole time nonstop. It was really remarkable. He would dominate the whole floor. He was that guy on the dance floor that you couldn't turn your eyes from," remembers Michelle. "Matt danced in a way I had never seen anyone dance before. He would go from side to side in these huge sweeping motions. He demanded space on the dance floor. You couldn't stand next to him because he would knock you over. He was incredible. He would dance for hours and hours and come off the floor sopping wet from head to toe."

One night Matt left a club late at night to meet up with Michelle, showing up at her door with his left shoe missing.

"Matt, where is your shoe?" she asked.

Matt looked down at his bare sock, then looked back up at her, smiling. "I lost it dancing."

4

ABANDONMENT

B ehind the scenes, Matt Drudge's high school years were marked by increasing instability. Matt's parents had become aware of his sexuality. Matt later confessed to a friend that they didn't accept his lifestyle, and that they thought something was wrong with him.

While both of Matt's parents shared progressive values, most Americans and medical professionals in the mid-1980s were still grappling with how to come to terms with the issue of homosexuality.

Only fourteen years earlier, homosexuality was still listed as a mental disorder by the American Psychiatric Association. When in 1973 the American Medical Association voted to drop the label of homosexuality as a mental disorder, it replaced it with "sexual orientation disturbance for people in conflict with their sexual orientation," which was defined as a category "for individuals whose sexual interests are directed toward people of their own sex and who are either disturbed by, in conflict with, or wish to change their sexual orientation."

Popular culture was also sharply divided, often framing the concept of sexuality in moral terms. When asked by Gallup in 1982, "Do you think homosexual relations between consenting adults should or should not be legal?" only 45 percent of Americans polled answered "should be legal," whereas 39 percent answered "should not be legal."

Matt's "mental health issues" corresponded with the continual deterioration of his mother's health, according to the Maryland Court Archives. In April 1982 Claire suffered a severe toxic reaction to a medication that caused her to be hospitalized. In June, Claire told the court, "I returned home, where I remain under doctor's care. I have no financial means with which to meet Matthew's special and urgent needs."

With nowhere left to turn, Claire sent Matt to live with his father in Tyaskin, Maryland, on a soybean farm with his father's new wife and her two sons. But after three weeks, the teenager was sent back to live with his mom.

According to Claire, "Robert Drudge rejected his natural son, Matthew, and returned him to my home, knowing that I am under doctor's care and unemployed. His reason for returning Matthew to me after three weeks was that his wife comes first; her two boys come second, and Matthew comes third, that he did not assume any responsibility for him as his father because he has a new family; that he hopes everything turns out all right. Robert Drudge has not communicated with his son or me since that time."

She continued, "As a result of these experiences, I believe that Matthew will require special attention in the form of psychiatric and social services as well as social educational services."

———

After returning back to his mother's care, records show that his treatments increased. In 1982 Matt received a "psychological evaluation," a "psychiatric evaluation," and at least twelve "individual psychotherapy sessions" at the Jewish Social Agency in Rockville, Maryland.

By September 15, 1982, Matt's "emotional problems" had escalated. This time Matt was admitted into the facility for an extended stay as part of a psychological evaluation. It concerned Matt's dad enough to provoke a rare visit.

"Matt told me he had pneumonia and that was the reason he was away," remembers Michelle.

———

By his senior year Matt Drudge had delivered his last newspaper for the *Washington Star*. After 128 years, the paper filed for bankruptcy and was forced to sell its property to its competitor, the *Washington Post*. Matt got a new job bagging groceries at the Giant in nearby Wheaton Plaza.

And he continued dancing. Always until dripping with sweat from head to toe. Often all night.

As graduation was nearing, Matt told friends that he hadn't bothered applying for colleges. That he "knew he wouldn't do well."

Matt would later sum up his time in public education: "I don't like authority and I didn't like structure. My expertise in high school was cutting classes. Boy I knew how to do that. I never got caught. I got suspended a few times."

In 1984 Matt graduated from Northwood High School ranked 341st out of 355 students.

In his Arrowhead yearbook, he dedicated his senior quote, a mock "last will and testament" to Michelle. "To my true friend Ms. Thing VickyB I leave a night in Paris, a bottle of Chaps cologne and hope you find a school with original people—and to everyone else who has helped and hindred [sic] me whether it be Staff or students, I leave a penny for each day I've been here and cried here. A penny rich in worthless memories. For worthless memories is what I have endured. It reminds me of a song, 'The Funeral Hyme [*sic*].'" He ended with his personal motto: "Where there's a will, there's a way."

5

INTERNET

While America was still basking in the afterglow of its postwar superiority, on the morning of October 4, 1957, transmitters first picked up a strange noise from above. By that afternoon, the nation's confidence and optimism would come plummeting down to Earth in a cascade of ominous newspaper headlines that spread across the evening editions being hawked at busy street corners or hand-delivered to homes across the country.

RUSSIANS WIN RACE TO LAUNCH EARTH SATELLITE read the headline from United Press correspondent Daniel F. Gilmore.

The article began, "The pulsating radio 'beep' of the first man-made earth satellite signaled today to the world that man had crossed the threshold into the age of travel through space."

The article continued, "Launching of the satellite was a tremendous victory for science. It was a more tremendous victory for Soviet propaganda to be able to trumpet to the world the Russians were the first to break through the frontiers of space."

The American citizenry weren't the only ones shocked by the Russian success in launching Sputnik into Earth's orbit. President Dwight Eisenhower and his administration had found themselves caught flat-footed. The president convened his Science Advisory Committee to solicit opinions from America's brightest minds on how best to answer this new development in the ongoing Red Scare. He emerged from the meeting with a harsh warning for the American people: unless the nation mobilized, it would lose its scientific and technological lead.

Three months later, Eisenhower ordered the creation of the Advanced Research Projects Agency (ARPA). Serving under the Department of Defense and with unprecedented power, ARPA was granted a $520 million appropriation with a $2 billion budget plan and given discretion over all US space programs and advanced strategic missile research. In January 1958 America pushed back with the launch of Explorer 1, propelling the United States into the space race.

It would give the public just a small glimpse of the technological advances to come. Over the next four years, the agency would embark on a mission to assemble the best technical and scientific minds that could be found in American research. On top of that list was Joseph Licklider, an associate professor at MIT. A philosopher more than a technician, Licklider had helped establish a cutting-edge psychology program for engineering students that challenged the conventional wisdom of the day. Not only would Licklider help America reclaim the lead in the space race, but through his fearless innovations, he would begin to plant the seeds that would become the World Wide Web.

Computers were regarded as nothing more than giant calculators in 1962, when Licklider was tapped to run ARPA's new behavioral science department. Typical of these early models was the Mark I, a fifty-one-foot-long, eight-foot-tall switchboard created by Harvard mathematics professor Howard Aiken in 1944 as an "analytical engine" to compute and print mathematical tables. The machine was considered ahead of its time and was employed by researchers trying to determine whether implosion was a viable choice to detonate the atomic bomb during World War II.

But Licklider arrived on the scene touting a revolutionary idea. Instead of seeing computers as high-powered supercalculators, he had the broader vision of viewing electronic circuitry as potential extensions of the whole human being, and as a tool that "could amplify the range of human intelligence and expand the reach of our analytical powers."

When Bob Taylor, a young program officer from NASA, took over as the agency's director in 1965, he found the process of exchanging new data with the agency's satellite research communities tedious and time consuming. Taylor was determined to find a way to connect all the different machines. But how?

A breakthrough came a year later when in 1966 American scientist Paul Baran discovered a new way of grouping all transmitted data into sized blocks, called packets. Baran's concept, "distributed adaptive message block switching," would provide an efficient routing method for sending messages, allowing multiple users to communicate over a single network.

The discovery was a game changer. By 1969 the first data exchange over this new network occurred between computers at UCLA and the Stanford Research Institute. It didn't go well. On their first attempt to log in to Stanford's computer they needed to type "log win," but after typing the letter g, the UCLA researchers' computer crashed. But the failure would set the stage for future successes as the technology continued to grow throughout the 1970s before making another leap on January 1, 1983, when researchers began to assemble what soon became called "the network of networks," allowing computers from around the country to share information.

By 1990 what had once been a small community of a few thousand computer scientists, engineers, and programmers who quietly shared their online data had suddenly been flooded by millions of newcomers. Now anyone with a personal computer and a modem could easily and inexpensively gain access to the global web of computer networks.

Thousands of online bulletin boards through systems like Usenet on networks such as BITNET and Internet popped up across the country, allowing users to exchange information and share opinions. Just as quickly, controversy sprung up over who was responsible for the new medium. Prodigy, a board run by Sears and IBM, eliminated from its bulletin a section called "Health Spa" after a heated electronic debate broke out about homosexuality. Stanford University officials barred student access to a national electronic joke book after complaints about ethnic slurs.

Privacy concerns arose on another board after a city councilman was discovered to have been reading private messages between users. In an editorial in the *New York Times* responding to heated online conversations, the paper opined that the networks "are essentially like telephone lines: responsibility for the content of any of the hundreds of bulletin boards rests with the originator of the discussion."

The article quotes one expert as saying, "When we talk on the phone, you can listen to my tone of voice . . . Opinions read off the computer carry a stronger message than if the same thing were said face to face . . . The result is a phenomenon that computer experts call 'flaming'—the electronic version of an out-of-control shouting match." "Flaming can reach incredibly nasty levels," wrote Eugene Spafford, an assistant professor of computer science at Purdue University. "If there was the equivalent of an electronic bullet, you'd see them fly."

———

Despite the concerns, the information superhighway was spreading like wildfire, eclipsing all other technologies that had preceded it. While it took radio thirty-eight years to attract fifty million listeners and TV thirteen years, once available to the public, the internet reached fifty million users in four years.

In 1993 the National Center for Supercomputer Applications in Champaign, Illinois, which had launched a new service called the World Wide Web to serve as an electronic library, saw the number of daily queries rise from one hundred thousand requests in June to almost four hundred thousand just four months later.

In 1993 the *Cyber Sleaze Report*, MTV VJ Adam Curry's electronic gossip sheet that carried details about Madonna's private life and other newsy tidbits about the entertainment industry, drew so many views that the Panix Public Access Network told Curry he had to set up his own host computer with his own internet address. He did. It was called MTV.com.

By 1994 the internet had officially arrived as a pop culture phenomenon.

"What is internet, anyway?" a confused Bryant Gumbel asked Katie Couric in a January 1994 segment of the *The Today Show*.

"Internet is that massive computer network," answered Couric. "The one that's becoming really big now."

Couric wasn't the only one who thought something big was happening.

———

Paul Saffo, a computer industry consultant at the Institute for the Future, a research firm based out of Menlo Park, California, told the *New York Times*, "Think of this as television colliding with the telephone party line . . . In terms of social consequences, the Web is a great experiment. It's going to deliver us community with a vengeance—and we may find we don't want it."

Silicon Valley entrepreneur Steve Kirsch also saw the potential and announced plans to launch Infoseek, which he described as a commercial version of the free internet by acting as a clearinghouse for newspapers and other electronic publishers, which would bill customers based on their use of the network.

Geocities.com, a site founded in 1994 that allowed users to build their own home pages, was growing in popularity. Now, for the first time, user-generated content was available to the mainstream.

By November 1995, the Associated Press announced it would begin distributing its articles and photographs over the World Wide Web.

The news-gathering service was originally created in 1846 by a group of publishers who believed that a new technology of the time, the telegraph, could speed the collection of and dissemination of information. Now the media entity saw the internet as the next step in the global spread of information. In an article appearing in the *New York Times* on November 20, 1995, John Markoff wrote, "It was simply the latest, but perhaps most historically significant, move yet by an old-line media organization into the World Wide Web, the internet multimedia information-retrieval system that appears on the verge of becoming a mass medium itself."

The new technology wasn't looked at as a competitor, but instead as a tool that could help existing media flourish. Markoff continued, "Its complementary role is already evident: many radio stations and all the major television networks have Web sites promoting their programs and stars. Newspapers, including the *New York Times*, are devising cyberspace editions."

Most important, the article concluded, "For very little money, and with a modicum of computer skills, virtually anyone can create his or her own Web site. Anyone with a modem is potentially a global pamphleteer."

6

NEW YORK CITY

From all outward appearances, Matt Drudge's post–high school future appeared bleak.

The young man from a broken home had barely graduated high school and hadn't even considered higher education. But with Chaka Khan and Afrika Bambaataa pumping through the headphones of his Walkman and hip-hop lyrics scrawled in black marker on his white Converse high-tops, Matt was exuding optimism as he browsed through the vinyl covers at 12" Dance Records at P Street in Dupont Circle, Washington, DC.

It was that swagger that first caught the attention of local high school senior Craig Seymour. Through their mutual love of music, and the soap opera *The Young and the Restless*, they struck up an easy friendship.

The two got jobs working as telemarketers, hawking Time-Life's Old West book series to retirees. After finishing the day shift, they would walk to Connecticut Avenue where Matt would stop at the Newsroom, a popular newsstand featuring hundreds of different magazines and newspapers. There, Matt would pull pieces of paper out of his pockets and take notes. It was like he was back on his Takoma Park bench, but instead of the *Washington Star* and the *Unicorn Times*, he worked his way through newspapers and magazines from around the world.

"Matthew was one of those people who was always obsessed with the news. And with minutiae. Mostly about the entertainment industry," says Seymour. "He would write down bits of information on all these scraps of paper."

Late at night, Matt would often call Seymour and share the observations he had gleaned from that day's trip to the Newsroom.

"He could call me any time of day or night to tell me about some weird news going on at CBS News or something that had caught his eye from record charts," recalls Seymour. "Matt always knew a lot of interesting things, and he liked that other people knew that."

———

Matt never seemed hobbled by his academic failings, instead projecting to those around him the sense that he was on the cusp of greater things.

In Seymour's words, "He would always talk about how he didn't want to start at the bottom, like he knew enough, and was smart enough that someone should pay for his opinion. Even though he was young, Matt never thought of himself as an intern or anything like that. He would say, 'I really feel like I am at the point where someone should be paying me for my thoughts.'"

Some nights the two road-tripped to New York City. Their mission was to stake out music producers.

"Matt didn't care about the stars. His interest was always in the people behind the curtain. The ones with the real power," says

Seymour. "Matt was a person who was interested in money. But he didn't crave fame. He wanted a certain type of notoriety. He didn't want to be in the public eye. All the people he admired were the people who worked their power behind the scenes."

Together, Matt and Seymour researched and found the addresses of different studios. Once there, they waited outside for hours, hoping to bump into one of their favorite producers coming or going. One night they hit gold when they found producer Arthur Baker, who was best known for his work with the British group New Order. The duo approached Baker, but Matt didn't ask for an autograph. He only wanted to express his admiration.

"Matt wanted to get as close to big people because he believed they would recognize his talent," says Seymour. "That they would see that something special inside of him."

Matt's self-confidence manifested outwardly in the form of an upbeat and charismatic persona to his small pocket of friends, according to Seymour, but his obsessiveness over news, and especially the entertainment business, could sometimes put people off.

"He was never into casual conversation. I was one of the few people who tolerated that because it would get on most people's nerves," says Seymour. "But he knew information about such a broad range of topics that he could engage anyone. And he did."

One day, while driving back to their apartment, the issue of sexuality came up when Seymour, who at the time was closeting his homosexuality, told Matt that he couldn't imagine kissing another guy. Matt responded without hesitation, "Of course you can."

That moment changed Seymour's life: "It was one of those amazing moments where he saw something in me I couldn't even see myself. And by saying that he was making it OK for me and almost giving me permission to be myself. I will always appreciate that. Matt was a very good friend. He would push me to do the things he thought I should be doing, always encouraging me to do more to expand my possibilities."

After a few months, Matt and Seymour moved closer to New York City. They wanted to be around the "great people." They leased an apartment with a few friends on Grove Street in Jersey City, New Jersey. Matt got a job at a local grocery store stocking shelves. When after a few months it had become clear that Jersey wasn't where the action was, they moved to a cramped walk-up apartment on 14th Street in Manhattan. Matt got a job at McDonald's and continued to spend his free time perusing newsstands, making notes, going to record stores, and dancing the night away at Heartthrob and Club 1018. But his time in New York City would be short-lived.

One of the female roommates had developed a crush on Matt, and the feelings weren't mutual. And as tensions in the apartment began to rise, Matt found himself in a relationship with a man he had met in New York City, and it had turned abusive.

"Matt kept what was going on to himself, but we knew it wasn't good," a friend remembers.

Matt had nowhere to turn. His mom was struggling with mental illness, and his dad had all but disowned him. Michelle hadn't heard from Matt in several months. She had become worried and decided to reach out. Matt answered the phone, sounding panicked.

"Hey, I've been trying to reach you. How are you doing, Matt?" she asked.

Matt answered, "Well, I'm getting my ass beat by my boyfriend, and I have no place to go. So that's about it, so, bye."

He hung up on her.

After just a few months, Matt fled the New York City apartment in the middle of the night. He didn't tell anyone, not even Seymour, where he was going.

Seymour recalls, "We just woke up and Matt was gone."

7

TALK RADIO

On June 24, 1994, President Bill Clinton, while traveling back from a D-day commemoration in France, called into KMOX, a St. Louis radio station, in order to vent. His specific target: talk radio.

"I think there is too much cynicism and too much intolerance," he said of the American public. "But if you look at the information they get, if you look at how much more negative the news reports are, how much more editorial they are and how much less direct they are, if you look at how much of talk radio is just a constant, unremitting drumbeat of negativism and cynicism, you can't—I don't think the American people are cynical, but you can't blame them for responding that way."

In the twenty-three-minute interview, Clinton denounced what he called "violent personal attacks." He used the word "cynical" or "cynicism" ten times.

The push and pull between politicians and radio hosts dates back nearly to radio's inception—on February 6, 1924, at 8:00 p.m. Pacific time, thirty-four-year-old preacher Aimee Semple McPherson stepped before a large microphone in the heart of Los Angeles.

McPherson's charismatic sermons denounced everything from the teaching of evolution and jazz music, which she called "the work of the Satan," to corruption in government, especially law enforcement.

Listeners of early American radio had never heard anything like it. The only connection to the outside world most of them had ever known came from the booming print newspaper market. In fact, in 1924 there were 2,042 English-language dailies in 1,295 American cities with a total circulation of 27.8 million. Many households took morning and evening papers, which usually cost two cents. Most cities had papers with different ownerships and editorial policies— usually Republican or Democrat.

But the public had become quickly hooked on radio as the pro-gressive evolution in technology made radio sets more affordable to an increasing number of Americans. By the mid-1920s, a radio set could be found in the living room of most middle-class American homes.

Soon, others joined McPherson in the counterculture radio revolution—most notably Father Charles Coughlin. A Canadian American Roman Catholic priest based near Detroit at the National Shrine of the Little Flower Basilica in Royal Oak, Michigan, Coughlin began his radio broadcasts in 1926 with a focus on the applications of the Catholic faith.

When Coughlin began veering into politics, often devoting long monologues in support of presidential nominee Franklin D. Roosevelt during the election of 1932, the candidate happily used the popular radio host to his advantage. But two years into the New Deal, Cough-lin turned into a thorn in Roosevelt's side as his soft-spoken support turned into outspoken criticism of his policies that was often tinged with anti-Semitism.

Privately, the president worried that Coughlin's wide influence posed a serious threat to his administration's policies, and he was right to be worried. At his height, Coughlin had nearly one-third of America tuning in to his broadcasts, easily dwarfing the audience of Roosevelt's fireside chats, his own series of evening radio addresses.

In 1934, in an effort to wrest control of the airwaves, Roosevelt created the Federal Communications Commission. His administration argued that because there were only a limited number of broadcast stations and those available were in such great demand, the airwaves belonged in the public domain. However, it wouldn't take long for the regulatory agency to be used as a tool to reign in Coughlin and other voices of dissent.

First came the Mayflower doctrine, which declared that "broadcasters have an obligation to allot a reasonable amount of time to treatment of controversial issues and that they have an affirmative duty to seek, to provide representative expression of all responsible shades of opinion." FCC chairman Larry Fly said the move was necessary, "fearing a further commercialized, conservative-biased, and corporate dominated medium."

In July 1938 Elliott Roosevelt, the president's son, let Coughlin know how this new federal power could be weaponized to silence him.

> I dislike censorship in any form but even censorship might not be too high a price to pay if it will help insulate us against the anti-Semitic oratory of the radio priest out in Royal Oak, Michigan. For thirteen years this man's political fidelity has been as unpredictable as the wind . . . Just what effect the recently adopted code for broadcasters will have for Father Coughlin cannot be foretold at this time. In any case, it will be interesting to watch.

The radio industry fought back, insisting that the Mayflower doctrine was censorship and a violation of free speech. But when America entered World War II in 1941, government censorship of the media became widely tolerated by the American public in the name of helping the effort overseas.

After the war, broadcasters began once again to push back against the Mayflower doctrine, framing it as an infringement of their First Amendment rights.

Public sentiment was on the side of radio station owners, and the Mayflower doctrine was repealed in June 1949. But the FCC struck back later that year with a new regulatory policy much like the old one, but under a new name—the fairness doctrine, which once again placed the content of radio broadcasts under the control of the FCC. The policy declared that holders of broadcast licenses present controversial issues of public importance in a manner that was—in the FCC's view—"honest, equitable, and balanced."

Congress backed the policy in 1954, and by the 1970s the FCC called the doctrine the "single most important requirement of operation in the public interest—the sine qua non for grant of a renewal of license."

For radio station owners, finding equal time for opposing views in a way that was both profitable and satisfied the vague regulatory statute proved difficult. An audience in the heart of Texas might tune in to a two-hour block of conservative views but would quickly turn the dial at the first sound of a liberal voice. Likewise, a liberal audience would quickly tune out a conservative voice in left-leaning San Francisco. As a result, most station owners found it easier to bow out of political talk altogether.

But by the mid-1980s, advances in technology and the expanding number of stations made it clear that there was no longer a scarcity of broadcast outlets, poking a hole in the premise of the FCC's justification for imposing the doctrine. President Ronald Reagan's administration decided to reexamine the issue, and Congress directed the FCC to examine alternatives to the fairness doctrine and to submit a report. Reagan's advisers warned that striking down the doctrine would unleash an already-antagonistic media against him, but the president saw the policy as a clear violation of constitutional rights.

In 1985 CBS-TV's Dan Rather testified in an open hearing before the FCC. "When I was a young reporter, I worked briefly for wire services, small radio stations, and newspapers, and I finally settled into a job at a large radio station owned by the *Houston Chronicle*. Almost immediately on starting work in that station's newsroom, I became aware of a concern which I had previously barely known existed—the FCC. The journalists at the *Chronicle* did not worry about it; those at the radio station did . . . Once a newsperson has to stop and consider what a government agency will think of something he or she wants to put on the air, an invaluable element of freedom has been lost."

On August 5, 1987, the FCC voted to overturn the fairness doctrine 4–0. Democratic attempts to pass legislation to sidestep the agency by giving the regulation the force of law were thwarted after Reagan vetoed the legislation.

With the radio waves unchained, the stage was now set for an explosive new voice: Rush Limbaugh.

Limbaugh's radio career began at the age of sixteen when in 1967, using the name Rusty Sharpe, he worked a series of disc jockey jobs. In 1979 he took a break from the airwaves, but in 1984 he was back, landing a talk show at the Sacramento, California radio station KFBB, replacing Morton Downey Jr. With the fairness doctrine gone, and stations beginning to do away with the general advice chat shows in exchange for large blocks of programming, it opened the door for more political talk . . . and Limbaugh.

By tapping into the frustration of a growing number of people who felt their points of view were being underrepresented, Limbaugh was able to offer an alternative narrative to the one being offered by the print media or the Big Three: ABC, CBS, and NBC.

Daniel Henninger wrote, in an editorial in the *Wall Street Journal*, "Ronald Reagan tore down this wall [the fairness doctrine] in

1987 . . . and Rush Limbaugh was the first man to proclaim himself liberated from the East Germany of liberal media domination."

Limbaugh believed that the majority in this country were being misrepresented by the mainstream media and had data to back up his argument. In a 1988 Gallup poll, people identified as conservative or liberal at a ratio of 2:1, whereas more than 90 percent of the journalists and newscasters had donated money to the Democratic Party.

And Limbaugh's audience agreed. Listeners across the country tuned into Limbaugh in unprecedented numbers. In 1988 Limbaugh began broadcasting his show nationally from radio station WABC in New York City.

———

The rise of Limbaugh marked another significant shift in the media landscape. The end of the fairness doctrine had freed talk radio, decentralizing debate and information—both good and bad—to the extent that even the most powerful man in the free world was having trouble competing.

By June 24, 1994, Rush Limbaugh had an audience of twenty million listeners a week, a television show, a bestselling book in the works, the courtship of aspiring presidential candidates, and the commander in chief calling him out publicly as a threat to democracy from Air Force One.

Limbaugh, President Clinton noted to St. Louis radio station KMOX, would have three hours on his own program later in the day "to say whatever he wants."

"Would you like to leave a message?" Clinton was asked by the interviewer.

The president responded that he didn't have a message for the radio host. He wanted the public to understand the disadvantage he was at. The bully pulpit of the American presidency couldn't compete with what he called an "unprecedented attack" from the airwaves.

Listeners could hear anger boiling over in Clinton's voice as he vented over how the narrative had been seized by a man behind a microphone. A man unrestrained by regulation, accountable only to his listening public. "I won't have any opportunity to respond, and there's no truth detector. You won't get on afterwards and say what was true and what wasn't!"

Two days later Limbaugh got behind the microphone and did just that.

"I AM the truth detector," he began.

8

HOLLYWOOD

After having fled his New York City apartment in the middle of the night, Matt Drudge moved back to Takoma Park, Maryland, where the chaos he had left behind was waiting for him. His mother continued to be plagued with health problems and his relationship with his father was nonexistent.

Matt got a job as a night manager at 7-Eleven in nearby Gaithersburg. He would later remember his job at the convenience store for giving him a head start on that day's headlines.

"Every morning at about 2 o'clock the bulldog editions of all the major papers would be dropped off right at my doorstep," he would later write. "I couldn't wait to get my hands on them. While the rest of the city slept, I'd read fresh headlines and bylines—first, before anyone else."

Matt studied the papers and saved his paychecks. Six months after leaving the apartment, he wrote to his friend Seymour, "If this letter gets to you somewhere in this burning world, I have a feeling you can still relate."

Matt wrote in the letter about music, his anticipation of the new Frankie Knuckles (a popular DJ known as the "Godfather of House Music") remix, and lamented over the fate of his favorite show, *The Young and the Restless*: "The show suffered so much over the writer's strike—will it ever rebound?" Later, he stated, "Writing this letter to you makes me happy. Whatever happened to us? I miss talking to you, but somehow I know what you're thinking or want to convince myself that I know." .

Matt ended the letter with a clue to his next move. "213 area code soon. Call me."

In 1987 Matt moved again, this time leaving Takoma Park for Los Angeles, where he found a small one-bedroom apartment for $600 in a section of Hollywood "they're always promising to clean up but never do." He adopted a six-toed cat named Cutie. From his ninth-floor apartment at the corner of Hollywood and Vine, Matt found himself in the entertainment capital of the universe . . . with a view of CNN's local headquarters and the high-rise where E! Entertainment's offices were located.

Matt's goal in Los Angeles was the same as it had been in New York City. He knew he had ability. He believed he understood more about the entertainment agency than the writers covering the beat, so now all he needed was for someone to notice.

He walked the famed Sunset Strip, sometimes stopping at Ronald Reagan's brass star on the Hollywood Walk of Fame to wipe the epithets off, or at World Book & News at the corner of Hollywood and Cahuenga to note any interesting tidbits. One day, while perusing the news rack, Matt spotted an advertisement in *Variety* for a job as a runner for the game show *The Price Is Right*. He interviewed and got the job. The pay was five dollars an hour.

The job proved fortuitous. Not only did it earn him enough money to pay his rent and afford his steady diet of thirty-nine-cent tacos, but it also gave him his first real glimpse into Hollywood. And Matt was finally being noticed. He soon impressed his bosses at the game show and was promoted to the CBS Studios gift shop. Once there, he was bumped up the ladder again, this time to assistant manager, where he became responsible for all the books and purchasing. The higher-ups were so enamored of his work ethic that they flew him from Hollywood to New York City to show CBS's New York employees how to expertly manage their store.

The job also proved a perfect setting for the aspiring journalist. The building teemed with Hollywood power brokers, and through his position, Matt did whatever it took to place himself in their path. Suddenly, Matt found himself in the orbit of some of the world's biggest stars, from Jerry Seinfeld to Roseanne Barr, who both ran their top-rated shows out of the Studio City lot. Matt chatted up everyone he saw and began stockpiling information. He volunteered in the CBS mailroom and intercepted memos.

"I went out of my way to service executive suites, listening carefully to whispered conversations, intercepting the occasional memo. Stalking the newsroom," he would later remember. Now more than ever, he felt like he was going places.

———

But being on the opposite coast didn't help Matt's family issues. Since leaving Takoma Park, Matt had told friends he kept his family at arm's length. He rarely spoke to his mom, who by 1992 had decided to leave a job she had taken at a local convenience store to volunteer helping to answer questions from the public in the new Clinton administration.

Matt's father, Robert, had married for a third time in 1989, this time to a woman named Rita Foust, also a Maryland native. Rita recalls that during their two years of marriage Robert didn't have a single interaction with Matt. She says she never asked Robert why the two never spoke, only that "it was a very strange family. Very reclusive."

But Robert did have a fixation that he would soon share with his son—computers. He had bought one in 1991 and had "spent hours messing around on it," according to Rita. "He got very into it," she says. "He took up programming and writing code and became very good at it."

By early 1994 Robert Drudge had reconnected with his son, paying a visit to his Los Angeles apartment. He became convinced that Matt was spinning his wheels at his gift shop gig. Robert hoped to jump-start his son's career, and possibly provide an outlet for him to focus his seemingly boundless energy and intellect.

"Matt's mind goes a thousand beats a second and then the next second there's something else," Robert would later say.

On the drive back to the airport after his visit, "sensing some action was needed," Robert made a detour to a strip mall off Sunset Boulevard. It was there that he purchased his son his first computer, a $1,500 486 Packard Bell. He thought it would be good for Matt to apply his mind to something new and different.

"Oh yeah," Matt thought. "What am I gonna do with that?"

9

GOSSIP

Zeitgeist is defined as "the spirit or mood of a particular period of history as shown by the ideas and beliefs of the time." In retrospect, historians often portray the mood of an era as a collective push toward an inevitable conclusion—a chain reaction of events set in place over centuries, or even millennia, until the planet's surface gives way to the pressure and cracks, unleashing a massive wave sweeping up the whole of society, pushing it forward and reshaping all in its wake.

American culture in the late '80s and mid-1990s was experiencing a renaissance of hope and renewal, marked by images of the Berlin Wall crumbling down, cheers echoing worldwide at the release of Nelson Mandela after his twenty-seven years in prison, and flashy neon posters of New Kids on the Block hanging on suburban bedroom walls. After twelve years of Republican leadership in the White

House, the youthful Bill Clinton, who had come out of nowhere and from nothing, galvanized thousands—dancing to the Fleetwood Mac song "Don't Stop" pumping through stadium speakers at the 1992 Democratic National Convention—and went on to be elected to the highest office.

Societal expectations were also evolving. Americans entering the workforce confronted a new blueprint for success as rules were rewritten and opportunities expanded beyond the traditional socio-economic boundaries of the past. Now, four-year colleges weren't just for the elite. They were for everyone. The rate of homeownership was climbing too. The wave was moving forward—and in its wake, American culture. Everyone would be taken along for the ride.

Or almost everyone.

———

Matt Drudge had made up his mind. It was a decision he had made consciously, he would later tell friends: He was not going to ride along. He was going to "create his own wave." To do this, he would draw from a different time for inspiration—the era of the trailblazers, when newspapers were still in their prime, especially that intersection where print news and scandal collided: the gossip pages.

He studied the work of Louella Parsons, the first American movie columnist and famed screenwriter. Parsons got her big break at the *Chicago Record-Herald* in 1941 when, after learning that all the stars of the day had to pass through Chicago on their way from New York to Los Angeles, she had the idea to go down to the train station and interview the stars during their two-hour wait for the next train. She figured they would be glad to have something to do, and from these meetings she could put together a column about their personal lives. The column was a hit and soon drew the attention of newspaper publisher William Randolph Hearst. Once syndicated, Parsons's fame went global. At her peak, her columns were read by twenty million people in four hundred newspapers worldwide.

But it was 1920s-era columnist Walter Winchell who would become Matt's biggest influence. Winchell had made a name for himself by printing private, often salacious, information about famous people for the struggling *New York Evening Graphic*. Readers couldn't wait to read about who was having an affair with whom or who in high society had recently become pregnant. When other publishers saw what Winchell's column was doing for circulation at the once-lowly *Graphic*, the gossip column became an important mainstay of the American newspaper, and by 1940, thanks to his column and radio show, Winchell was considered among the most powerful people in the world, with an estimated reach extending to 80 percent of the American public.

Matt would later acknowledge the columnist's influence, but with a caveat: "To me it's only the Winchell spirit that I'm gravitating toward, as opposed to the man. He put himself in the center of situations. I do just the opposite. I remove myself from the fray and monitor everything from above."

———

Matt had long understood that, for him, riding along with the wave would have resulted in a life of mediocrity. He aspired to something greater, and to do that he would need to bring the past into the future.

10

PRODIGY

Netscape opened. Check.
AOL username. Check.
Password. Check.
Dialing local access phone number.
Bzzzzzt . . . chirp . . . budeedledeedledeedlebip! . . .

From a small Hollywood apartment, amid the screech and fizz of a Packard Bell computer's dial-up modem handshake bouncing through wires, crossing states and oceans, twenty-nine-year-old Matt Drudge's penchant for snooping was about to pay off.

He had subscribed to Prodigy, an online service that offered access to weather, shopping, games, polls, expert columns, banking, stocks, travel, and news. But a revelation came one day after logging in to one of his favorite sources for news, the Associated Press.

Matt had grown up a student of print newspapers and had always operated under the assumption that each article was the same everywhere. But now, logged on to the Prodigy server, he could see there were multiple versions of the same Associated Press article, with many carrying alternative information and headlines.

For those in charge of the newspaper's layout, the system made perfect sense. The ability to choose among a range of versions allowed editors to cater their periodical to their diverse readerships, since subscribers to a small rural newspaper in Mooresville, Alabama, would have different tastes than readers of the *San Francisco Chronicle*. In the past, all these different copies of the same article had only been available to editors, but the internet gave Matt the same view as the national editors.

The more Matt studied, the more he became convinced that there was a flaw. The system gave editors the ability to shape perceptions on both a local and national scale by altering the articles. They could place a shorter version of a wire story that contained damaging information about a Democratic politician in the back of the paper or run a longer version of a story that contained equally damaging information about a Republican politician. This, in Matt's opinion, gave newspaper editors enormous influence in shaping a narrative in the public consciousness.

He believed too many editors weren't as interested in catering to the needs of their readers as they were in using the system as a tool to implement a left-wing political agenda.

"It became a thing with Matt," says a friend from the time. "He would analyze how editors would select different versions of the same story to run in small papers across the country and he would be like, 'Look at what they are doing!'"

In addition to the Associated Press, Matt also became obsessed with the early internet bulletin boards. The internet of 1994 was a free-for-all, a new medium born of individualism and brimming with unbridled excitement as people across the world began making connections that would have been indistinguishable from magic only a few years earlier.

Chat sites alt.rave, rec.art.poems, alt.christnet, and alt.sex.stories had all become favorite destinations for Matt. They were safe places where anyone could share their counterculture ideas anonymously. By logging in from the corner of his small Hollywood apartment, he was able to connect with people from around the world. And on the internet, Matt didn't need a journalism degree or a platform to publish his thoughts for others to see. Just a dial-up connection and something to say.

On weekends, Matt spent his nights exploring the Santa Monica Boulevard club scene and would often dance into the early hours until coming back home to his Packard Bell.

———————

The idea for the Drudge Report began circulating in his mind soon after his father gave him the computer. On February 14, 1994, Matt registered the domain "The Drudge Report."

Matt would later say he began posting for one reader: himself.

His first published thoughts on the internet were far from inspired.

"Hello from sex drenched Hollywood," he posted on Usenet on December 28, 1994. Later in the day, he would expand on the thought, posting, "We are so sex drenched here in Hollywood. 65% of us city dwellers have herpes."

Matt's next few online communications were on the topics of natural catastrophes, Hollywood, and sex. On December 29, 1994, Matt posted on the group ca.earthquakes:

The morning of the 7.4 Japan quake I was busy fingering Tako (my love).
And boy she was blushing. Revealing that the plates are feeding off each other!
Tako stands high above the Volcano's base. She is my life.

Tako tells me more about
the ways of life than any science student could!
Tako wants more lovers.
Finger her at finger quake@tako.wr.usgs.gov................

On January 29, 1995, Matt posted:

well...madonna has pulled the plug on the oscar night interview with barbara walters!
seems as though the thought of going wide ...with a serious
one on one...was to much to
take right now. and besides her manager said she was going
to loose to the
'lion king' songs..so why do it? Madonna will be replaced by
jim carey on the oscarnight cast..
hello from hollywood...

His first several posts were glib and largely void of content, but all
that was about to change.

———

Matt's shift at the CBS Studios gift shop put him in the same building
as some of Hollywood's most influential power brokers, but his first
big break came straight out of the garbage. Matt had been searching
through the trash cans on the ground-floor Xerox room when he
discovered the previous day's Nielsen ratings, not yet released to the
public, discarded below piles of trash.

The junked paper detailed the audience size for the network's
programming. For Matt, it was information gold, even if he didn't
exactly know what to do with the pilfered information.

"I don't know what I did with it; I guess we, me and my friends
knew *Dallas* had got a 35-share over *Falcon Crest*, but we thought
we were plugged in," he would later recall.

Matt studied the schedule of the cleaning crew. He learned there
was a short window of time in the morning after the Nielsen numbers

were tossed into the garbage by the executive suits and before the crew would arrive to shred it.

Matt took his dumpster-diving routine elsewhere—including to *Daily Variety*. He began posting the Nielsen ratings and other tidbits of information he learned on various internet newsgroups, including pilfering Friday night's box office take for newly released movies, which he would release the very next day, ahead of the studios.

Matt got another scoop after overhearing actress Cybill Shepherd declare she would only work with women. He posted it online.

In February 1995 Matt got an email from a stranger asking him to "add me to the list." Matt didn't have a list at the time, but at that moment he decided to begin one.

On March 9, 1995, he posted the following announcement to several Usenet groups:

> For a free copy of the "Drudge Report" send a request via e-mail to drudge@lainet.com. The Report covers the Entertainment industry, Poli-Video shows (political talk shows,) Talk Radio, and a cross section of things that the editor Matt Drudge is focusing in on. This weekly report arrives on Monday and is complimented with NEWS BREAKS as they occur. Already read by key players, this tip sheet will be sure to peak your interest.

To supplement his newsletter, Matt decided to use the five megabytes of disk space that came with his personal ISP to create his own webpage, "The Drudge Report." He used PaintShop Pro software to create the design with big tabloid headlines that were sometimes amplified by a flashing police light. Next, he added links to major newspapers, wires, and to all the columnists he viewed as interesting: from Arianna Huffington to Liz Smith. Now all he needed were more stories.

Matt got another big break when he heard that Jerry Seinfeld had cleared out his office on the set of the sitcom. He began asking questions and discovered the star was asking for $500,000 an episode, and then he obtained an executive memo outlining the offer.

Two days later, on March 11, 1995:

ROCK ROCK ROCK TO THE PLANET ROCK...DONT STOP
THE DRUDGE REPORT IS REPORTING THAT:
Jerry Seinfeld is going to make $500,000 a week.................
Bill Clinton is not the only American President in trouble..The
new Rob reiner film is a 'holly-mess'...
Jenny Jones has blood on her microphone....
CNN is moving conservative....
We issue every Monday and when we get 'breaks.'

Matt fired out his Seinfeld salary scoop to his email subscribers
and then posted it to two dozen of the most popular internet newsgroups. He also linked his newsletter to a URL, www.lainet.net/drudge.

From there, the Drudge Report newsletter and website began
growing as a one-stop shop for news junkies.

Matt would later tell Harry Knowles, creator of the movie buff
website Ain't It Cool News, how every reader was a potential source
for his website, and that "the internet is going to be the thing that
knocks off CNN."

For the next nine months, Matt posted his stories every Sunday
night. He asked readers to send ten-dollar donations. In the first year,
Matt received $6,300, enough to pay for his bills, rent, and two tele-
phone lines. Matt bought three twenty-seven-inch Sanyo televisions
for his home office and added a fax machine.

By March 1995 he was getting so many new scoops that he quit
his $30,000-a-year CBS job to dedicate himself full-time to the Drudge
Report. In May, Matt got a tip from a reader that "Connie Chung's just
been fired. She just doesn't know it yet." It would be six days before
the rest of the media picked it up.

Matt would later write, "I wrote The Drudge Report for one reader
for a while—a couple of readers—5, 10, 15 readers. I had a thousand—
the first couple of months I thought, oh, that peaked that out."

11

CABLE

n June 1994 media watchers were all asking the same question: Was the public witnessing the beginning of the end of the Cable News Network phenomenon?

The cable channel that had revolutionized television news in 1980 was finding it tough to compete by the very rules it had established, as rival networks began offering round-the-clock news coverage of their own.

Now the same video of the same event that used to be available only on CNN was everywhere. But the network had defied critics before. Pundits had pronounced the twenty-four-hour news channel dead on arrival from the moment it went live.

On Sunday, June 1, 1980, at 5:00 p.m., eastern time, the Cable News Network launched its inaugural broadcast with an introduction by its founder, forty-one-year-old Ted Turner: "We won't be signing off until the world ends.

"We'll be on, we'll be covering it live, and that will be our last, last event. We'll play the national anthem for one time on the first of June, and that's all. When the end of the world comes, we'll play 'Nearer My God to Thee' before we sign off."

With a small staff based out of its Atlanta headquarters, and with bureaus in Chicago, Dallas, Los Angeles, New York City, San Francisco, and Washington, DC, the network was offering the public something entirely novel: news on demand. As one of its first guests, President Jimmy Carter referred to the new network as an "exciting and historic thing," capable of delivering news in much greater depth.

But critics believed that the stage was set for the dramatic fall of its flamboyant owner. Turner had entered the American lexicon as the outspoken millionaire entrepreneur owner of the SuperStation WTBS, and as the fearless skipper who won the 1977 America's Cup race with his yacht *Courageous*. But with no experience in the news business, Turner was sailing into uncharted waters.

News divisions at ABC, CBS, and NBC all balked at Turner's audacity, believing there was absolutely no way a man with zero news experience could successfully offer six times the programming of the networks at one-fifth the cost. Others feared he would use the new network as his personal mouthpiece, while competitors derided it as the "Chicken Noodle Network" because of its meager funding, a paltry budget of $3 million a month . . . as well as its meager staff of three hundred employees.

Skeptics also pointed to the various established print and broadcast news channels, which were firmly entrenched as the public's trusted sources for information. In 1980 the newspaper business was reaching new heights, with more than sixty-two million print papers in circulation across the United States. Millions more tuned in at 6:30 p.m., eastern time, to one of the Big Three (ABC, CBS, and NBC) to watch Dan Rather, Tom Brokaw, and Peter Jennings, all of whom had become national celebrities. It was a winning formula that had not been tinkered with since increasing their evening news programs in 1963, when they all went from fifteen- to thirty-minute segments.

Time Inc. and the *Washington Post* had both flirted with the idea of an all-news network, but dismissed it, believing that the available print newspapers combined with half an hour of television news every evening was already more than enough to satiate the public's appetite. Turner dismissed his television competitors as bores who were stuck in the past and the print newspapers as outdated relics:

The network nightly news is nothing more than a headline service. They don't offer business news, or sports news, and there is hardly any international news. I don't even watch it. Newspapers have traditionally provided the depth that television hasn't, but the fact is that newspapers are getting too expensive to produce and deliver. As energy sources run out, trees are becoming more precious. The Cable News Network will deliver a newspaper electronically and by the most efficient and inexpensive means available: satellite and cable.

———

Despite the bravado of its owner, CNN's first week of error-ridden broadcasts bordered on comical.

The *New York Times* wrote on June 5, 1980, that "nothing would be easier than compiling all the flubs experienced by CNN in its opening days. Among the more noticeable were missed cues, wrong name boards, lighting difficulties, and most of all, and ironically for a visual medium, audio foul-ups . . ."

Other publications lampooned the Cable News Network as "amateurish" and "not ready for prime time."

Turner pushed forward, holding firm to the belief that in time the network could build a loyal following by offering what the major networks did not—full and continuous coverage of all news events, both large and small. Its mantra was "Go live, stay with it, and make it important." He also saw a growing market of potential viewers. In 1980 sixteen million homes had cable, about twice as many as in 1973. He believed that trajectory would continue, boosting the number of eyes watching CNN along with it.

On January 1, 1982, Turner doubled down with the launch of CNN2, which later became known as CNN Headline News. The new network would broadcast a tightly formatted thirty-minute newsreel twenty-four hours a day, with freshly updated information that "briefly covered news, sports, entertainment, weather, and business."

Three years after its inception, Turner's gamble appeared to be paying off. In 1983 the all-news network turned its first profit. Viewership was on the rise. Twenty million homes (24 percent of all TV households) had access to CNN, while Headline News was being offered in another four and a half million homes (nearly 5 percent of TV households).

By November 1984 the Cable News Network had taken another jump, having increased its viewership to an average of 251,000 homes each day and was available to thirty million. When in September 1985 CNN began beaming its broadcast internationally, the network added 250,000 European homes to its viewership. The increased viewership allowed the network to bulk up its staff from 300 at its founding to nearly 1,500 employees, and its budget swelled from $36 million to $100 million a year.

———

But it was in the early hours of January 17, 1991, when the network *arrived*. Nearly six months after Iraq had invaded Kuwait, coalition forces, led by the United States, struck back, showering the Iraqi capital of Baghdad with cruise missiles. A CNN crew had gathered on the ninth-floor office in the Al Rasheed Hotel in Baghdad for a bird's-eye view of the destruction. It was a moment the network had prepared for months in advance.

Television satellite transmission equipment was not allowed into the highly controlled, secretive, authoritarian state, and the Iraqi government had told all journalists they would have to rely on filing reports from Iraqi state television facilities. However, the CNN producers believed that on day one coalition forces would strike the central Iraqi communications hub. The network decided to covertly construct two open parallel phone lines—one in each direction—to keep transmission capabilities open in the event of war.

It proved to be a stroke of genius. Stealth fighter jets destroyed Iraqi power and communications systems, leaving every other media company based in Baghdad without transmission capabilities. Only CNN was able to broadcast live—and they did, to hundreds of millions of people.

The coverage was as unprecedented as it was surreal. Viewers from around the world gathered around their television sets in the comfort of their living rooms to watch the first bombs drop in real time.

There was another first for the Cable News Network. While the Big Three had celebrity anchors reading from the teleprompters, at CNN the news had always been the star and the anchors largely anonymous, seemingly interchangeable with each other. Now, for the first time, CNN had its own media stars, with the cool and collected Bernard Shaw becoming an overnight pop culture phenomenon.

"The skies over Baghdad have been illuminated. We are seeing bright flashes going off all over the sky," Shaw told the captivated audience as explosions burst all around him.

CNN's war coverage not only won over critics but was also great for business. Ratings soared to a daily average of 3.8 to 4.2, from about 1 rating point before the war. "It's as though we were in training all this time for just this story," Ed Turner, the executive vice president of CNN, told the *New York Times*.

But the good ratings—like the changing news cycle—would prove to be short-lived.

By February 28, 1991, when General Norman Schwarzkopf had pulled his troops out of Iraq, CNN's audience left, too, in what would mark the beginning of a precipitous decline in viewership. Only three years removed from its unprecedented wartime coverage, the network's average prime-time audience hit rock bottom. In April and May of 1994 the channel's average audience in any given twenty-four-hour period fell to roughly 250,000 households, its lowest level since 1982.

But it wouldn't take long before the news cycle intervened yet again.

———

On November 7, 1994, Judge Lance Ito cleared the way for the live broadcast of O. J. Simpson's murder trial. Just months after posting near-record low numbers, viewers flocked to the Cable News Network for wall-to-wall coverage of the Simpson trial. For the first time, overall viewership for basic cable pulled even with the three major broadcast networks. By 1994, two-thirds of homes were equipped with cable television, and the Big Three were beginning to feel the heat.

"It's a little more like being pecked to death by ducks," one cable executive told the *New York Times*, "rather than eaten by a gorilla."

However, most analysts believed the new surge in ratings didn't represent a turning point for cable news but, instead, just another temporary blip. And there was another threat looming on the horizon. For the first time, CNN would soon be facing competition for the all-news, all-the-time market.

———

The official announcement of a joint venture between NBC and the Microsoft Corporation to create a new twenty-four-hour all-news cable channel to be named MSNBC came in December 1995, with *NBC Nightly News* anchor Tom Brokaw appearing on an enormous video screen live from an airfield in Ramstein Air Base in Germany. Across the room, on another screen, Bill Gates, the Microsoft chairman and CEO, appeared live by satellite from Hong Kong. The men held a satellite chat for the press to discuss how excited they were to partner in creating a new channel that would not only cover breaking news but also be complemented with the creation of an "interactive online news service."

Few took note that first reports of the scoop of NBC and Microsoft's venture didn't come from the *New York Times* media reporters. Or the *Wall Street Journal*. Or the *Washington Post*. Or the investigative staff at *NBC Nightly News*. Instead, they came from a little-known Hollywood-based blogger's weekly email newsletter.

12

ANDREW BREITBART

The red Geo Metro pulled up to the cottage in the Venice Canal Historic District section of Los Angeles on a typically sun-kissed day in March 1995. Matt Drudge stepped out from the car and onto the prestigious Carroll Canal Court.

The property he stood in front of belonged to the famous television actor and stand-up comedian Orson Bean and his wife, Alley Mills—who had become known to America as Norma Arnold, mother of Kevin Arnold in the coming-of-age series *The Wonder Years*. Waiting inside Bean's house was his daughter Susannah, along with her boyfriend, twenty-six-year-old Andrew Breitbart.

For Andrew, the moment had been years in the making. Born and raised in the wealthy Brentwood subsection of Los Angeles, Andrew never fit into the West Coast stereotype. For summer vacations, his parents would pack him and his sister, Tracey, into a thirty-two-foot motor home to trek across America. Out of the Los Angeles bubble, Andrew loved what he saw in flyover country.

Throughout his youth he had found himself immersed in the dominant political culture of his West Coast upbringing, viewing himself as a Bobby Kennedy–style liberal. But all that changed while watching the 1991 Clarence Thomas hearings, which were plagued by the controversial sexual harassment allegations of Anita Hill.

In an interview for C-SPAN, he commented years later,

> I watched day one, I watched day two, I watched the entire thing. I went from wanting him to be taken down to saying, "Where's the beef? What's going on here?"
>
> I don't understand what I'm watching here. I don't understand the color commentary that's on the screen, where they're saying, "Oh, this is outrageous." And I didn't understand the bumper stickers that were going by me on the streets that say, "I believe Anita." I believe Anita. What? What's going on here? My eyes were opened, perhaps for the first time, to the fact that something was awry in American political and media life.

The hearings left him feeling "deeply cynical of media that I thought were neutral and a Democratic Party I'd believed was guided by principle." He continued, "The national disgrace that was the Clarence Thomas confirmation hearings, for me, changed everything."

A jolt to his system, Breitbart began to reevaluate the left-leaning political axioms he had long taken for granted, opening his mind to other viewpoints. That's when he discovered Rush Limbaugh on KFI AM 640. For three hours a day, Limbaugh filled in the gaps of the pictures that had been forming in Breitbart's mind by analyzing the news of the day through the context of a collusion between the Democratic Party and the media that was trusted with presenting the facts. Breitbart coined it the "Democrat-media complex."

While coming to terms with his new political identity, Breitbart was struggling to find a career path when in 1992 a friend told him, "I've seen your future and it's the internet."

"What's the internet?" Breitbart answered.

———

Breitbart got his first computer, along with AOL and Prodigy on CompuServe, and eventually found himself in his apartment stacking chicken bones and bottles of pilsner, and logging on to the information superhighway. He took a job at E! Entertainment Television programming code, but for Breitbart, who suffered from attention deficit disorder, it wouldn't be long before he began wandering around the internet.

Once there, he realized he wasn't alone. In the dark corners of cyberspace, individual minds were liberated from conventional constraints. While their beliefs varied, they were united by the idea that something was wrong with society, that public education, Hollywood, and, most important, the media were disseminating bad ideas. On the internet, these like-minded cynics found their own world, far out of the reach of the mainstream, in alternative newsgroups like the Hollywood insider site alt.showbiz.gossip, the alien and conspiracy site alt.fan.artbell, and his favorite, the Clinton hate group alt.current-events.clinton.whitewater.

He became enamored of two regular posters who dominated the group. There was Wayne Mann, who compiled all the Clinton-related data he could get his hands on about Whitewater or any other rumored Clinton scandals and would share it with anyone who signed up for his email newsletter. The postings were chock-full of information about the ongoing case of Paula Jones, an Arkansas state employee who had alleged that she was sexually harassed by Clinton in a hotel room in 1991, while he was the governor of Arkansas.

The other person dropping information into the alt groups was Matt Drudge.

This Drudge character also had a news digest, but unlike Mann's singular focus on all things Clinton, the Drudge Report was an eclectic hodgepodge of information. As Breitbart would later describe, Matt would "have articles about the latest political scandal alongside articles on the upcoming election right next to articles on behind-the-scenes Hollywood business news, undercover contract talks, early revelations of box office data . . . all juxtaposed with earthquake and hurricane data. It was like a tour of one man's short-term memory."

Matt also had his share of politics, plunging headfirst down the Clinton conspiracy rabbit hole. It was there, down in the dark recesses of the internet, that Clinton wasn't only involved in shady land deals and bad mortgages but was also a drug dealer, rapist, and a murderer several times over. "I'm a Whitewater-a-holic," Matt would confess. "A Clinton crazy."

Breitbart subscribed to Matt's newsletter and began receiving the digest in his email inbox. Coupled with his steady diet of conservative talk radio, Breitbart's worldview continued to drift from the liberal principles of his youth.

"Reading the Drudge Report was opening my eyes to the power of the individual to take on massive, entrenched power—in government, the media, everywhere," Breitbart later wrote. "To borrow a phrase: Drudge was hope and change."

It wasn't just the newsletter that had piqued his interest. Breitbart had been fascinated by the man behind the Drudge Report. Matt seemed to know things, and he was using this new, unwieldy world of the internet to share unknown information about news, politics, and entertainment in a way unlike anyone else. And he was one man. He had no editor or staff, but with every new report his following grew in the fledgling corners of cyberspace. It seemed that every time Breitbart logged in, the name "Drudge" popped up.

"I came across the name Drudge so many times on the internet I didn't know whether he was a building, a news service, or an individual. Was Drudge an adjective or a noun? All I knew was that he was cutting through all the pretense," Breitbart would later write.

Breitbart sent Matt an email asking if he would be willing to meet.

"Are you 50 people? A hundred people? Is there a building?" Breitbart wrote.

To Breitbart's surprise, Matt wrote back, agreeing to get together. He would not be disappointed.

———

As Matt walked toward the front door of the Venice cottage, he was greeted by Andrew and his girlfriend, Suzie. They talked for hours, launching into their shared libertarian beliefs, culture, and especially the evolving information landscape. The world was on the cusp of a major revolution, Matt told Breitbart. The old guard was dying. A new disorderly chaos fueled by free-thinking individuals would take its place.

Matt pointed to the internet message boards and the success of Rush Limbaugh as evidence that the change they were waiting for had already arrived. It was evidence, Matt argued, that America was craving alternative viewpoints.

Matt pointed out that for decades the media had been tightly controlled by a small handful of corporations. Matt argued that people were no longer being represented by the media but instead by a small group of elites determined to shape the news rather than report it. In Matt's view, a revolution was in the works. A war over information.

And the battlefield would be the internet.

———

The message resonated with Breitbart, and meeting Matt would serve as a launching-off point to a new world. Breitbart believed a revolution was coming too. That it was real. And he wanted to be part of it—whatever it took.

Breitbart and Matt also felt a personal connection to each other. Breitbart, who had been adopted into a Jewish family, would later tell friends, "It is kind of weird that Drudge and I are both secular Jews who are interested in faith issues." In Breitbart, Matt saw someone with boundless energy, a skeptical worldview, and who shared a passion for headlines and news.

Matt offered him a 25 percent ownership of the Drudge Report, but insisted that as part of the deal Breitbart would have to leave his desk job at E! and commit full-time to the website. Breitbart loved the idea, but leaving a secure, full-time job for a fringe start-up on a platform no one even knew existed wasn't a plunge he could afford to take. He said no to the partnership but agreed to do whatever he could to help with the site.

There would be no contract. Breitbart and Matt made a handshake agreement. Breitbart would get up and update the page with fresh links from 9:00 a.m. to 3:00 p.m. Matt would pay him "what he could."

As he watched Matt drive away, Breitbart felt he was on the cusp of greatness. "I remember he putt-putted away, and I looked at my girlfriend, who is now my wife, and I said, that guy is going to change the world," Breitbart would later recall. "And I was right."

13

DON'T BE BORING

Conservative radio show host George Putnam and investigative reporter Chris Ruddy were already seated at a large round table at an upscale Italian restaurant when Matt Drudge arrived. As the drinks began to flow, Matt, who was a big fan of Putnam's talk show and would frequently call in as "Matt from Hollywood," began rattling off the top of his head the latest he had heard about the Clinton conspiracies before launching into a speech about the opportunity that was the internet . . . and his plans to utilize it.

"I was late to get online," says Ruddy. "I saw what Matt Drudge was doing and I said to myself, that is freaking amazing. That through this thing called the internet he could reach massive amounts of people. That it was the future. And that it was going to be revolutionary."

Matt had closely followed Ruddy's various investigations into the scandals that dogged the Clinton administration, but none more so than what became known as Fostergate. On July 20, 1993, the body of deputy White House counsel Vince Foster was found in Fort Marcy Park, and several Clinton-connected conspiracy theories emerged that the death wasn't the suicide authorities had claimed. The Foster "cover-up" quickly became a lightning rod for those on the right who believed the Clinton administration would cover up their corruption at any cost.

Ruddy's investigations fed into the right-wing narrative, charging that Foster had met with foul play in the White House itself, with his body then transported to the Virginia park. The clear implication was that someone very high up, maybe even President Clinton, had ordered a hit. It was the Drudge Report that first began circulating Ruddy's news stories on the Whitewater investigation on his email list.

"Matt Drudge had this tremendous vision. Before the internet, if you didn't write a story for the *New York Times*, no one saw your story," said Ruddy.

By the end of 1995, Matt bragged that his email list had ballooned to more than three hundred thousand subscribers. He promised Ruddy that it would only be the beginning, boasting, "I'm going to have a million, more than the *Washington Post*." Matt's prediction would prove modest as over the next twenty-four months the Drudge Report would grow from a niche website into a bona fide media newsmaker.

———

After being the first to report Seinfeld's salary demands and the impending departure of Connie Chung, Matt followed up by beating the mainstream media to report that Bob Dole had chosen Jack Kemp to be his running mate for the 1996 Republican nomination for president. Then he struck again with an exclusive report alleging that Steven Spielberg was being questioned by Whitewater investigators about Hillary Clinton's billing records.

And with each new exclusive banner in bold Helvetica italic type-face emblazoning the Drudge Report, Matt was gaining new sources and access. He was being invited to movie premieres. The Drudge Report correctly predicted that *The Bridges of Madison County* would be a hit and that Quentin Tarantino's *Four Rooms* would bomb.

"This town is so locked in," Matt told *Los Angeles* magazine. "You've got *Hard Copy* and *Entertainment Tonight*—who are allegiant to Paramount—and *Extra*, which is Warner Bros. There's not one person writing out here besides me who doesn't really write for a studio—not one."

Each new source translated into new exclusives. And the cycle continued, snowballing, as politicians and newsmakers increasingly began to see the Drudge Report as a useful tool to get their message out.

"I feel like a fisherman on a lake with the most amazing fish," Matt said. "I've got thousands of people working for me that are stringers, that are emailers, that are eyewitnesses from the scene."

On November 12, 1996, Matt struck a deal with Wired.com, a website that focused on emerging technologies and culture, to begin syndicating the Drudge Report. Now that Matt's work was being reposted on one of the web's early titans, his audience would reach new heights.

Other media were taking notice, too—even if they didn't always acknowledge it. An exclusive piece published in the Drudge Report claiming that the movie *Titanic* was set to be the most expensive movie ever produced was picked up by CNN, who attributed it to "Hollywood sources." But it wasn't just that Matt was breaking stories—it was the kind of stories he was dropping. Nothing appeared off-limits: everything from monetary policy to the filming of a new "Gen Y version of *Romeo and Juliet*" in which seventeen-year-old actress Claire Danes agreed to do nude scenes. Matt reported that the filming was moved to Mexico, asking his readers if that was "perhaps an effort to evade American pornography laws." Nothing was sacred. There was just one rule: don't be boring.

———

The brilliance of DrudgeReport.com was its simplicity. In the beginning, there were no advertisements or pop-up videos—just what the editor decided was the top news of the moment, cycling at the speed of Matt's boundless energy.

Click on the site and the eye immediately gravitates beneath the DRUDGE REPORT logo at the top of the screen to the lead story in simple black all-caps Arial typeface over the white background of the large banner headline. Sometimes the letters are italicized. Sometimes not. And if the editor judged something to be of particular importance, a simple flashing siren, reminiscent of '80s-era Atari graphics, would appear.

Below the banner, there are three columns of black font headlines from all across the country, and organized in no particular order, with headlines randomly appearing and disappearing at the editor's discretion. The disorder creates a sense of adventure as the eye scans up and down, never knowing what to expect next. There could be a link to an impending hurricane threatening the Florida panhandle, followed by a link to a disappointing box office number of the most recent Tarantino film, and then the latest way-too-early poll numbers, and then to the right a link to a story about a giant snake found under the kitchen floorboards of a shocked Texas homeowner, above a story about a dramatic currency fluctuation in a small African country.

Beneath the headlines are links to the world's most interesting columnists from all political persuasions, as well as links to the newswires and prominent websites and news agencies.

Below the far-right column, toward the bottom of the page, is a small empty tip box, email address, and stats showing the number of "visits to Drudge."

In its simplicity there was a core functionality and usability to the site that made it accessible to even the most tech-illiterate consumers. All it took was a hover of the mouse over a headline, column, or news agency, a click, and then in the speed of cyberspace, readers were carried to news sites from all around the world.

An aura of drama enveloped the Drudge Report. Consumers of news could leave the site on their screen and know that at any moment a breaking-news update could splash across the screen. A new catchphrase quickly began spreading at dining room tables, watercoolers, and newsrooms throughout the country: "Did you see what's on Drudge?"

Aesthetically, the Drudge Report was truly unique. An absolute original. There was no other site in the world like it.

In the fall of 1996 Matt found his first national media exposure when he was interviewed by *Newsday* media writer Rita Ciolli, who had been watching how online media was changing journalism and had signed up for Matt's emails. "I was fascinated by his reports, especially on old media," says Ciolli.

During their phone interview Matt opined at length about two of his heroes, Ronald Reagan and Walter Winchell. "Matt loved what Walter Winchell represented in breaking through and becoming the most powerful person. He saw that as a model and was smart enough to understand the technology that was coming and splice them together," Ciolli observes.

Ciolli was also struck by Matt's disdain for what he considered the dishonesty of the traditional media, especially when it came to reporting about itself. "His independence was very important to him. He saw all the warts that went into mainstream journalism and couldn't stand the thought of anyone controlling his product."

The article began, "Walter Winchell invented the modern gossip column and Matt Drudge is reinventing it for the future . . .

Unbelievable as it may seem in the present age of telling all, there was a time when the press, in the name of good taste, was afraid to examine private lives."

She continued, "Drudge, like Winchell before him, catches the public's attention with wit, humor, and gimmicky presentations about the Washington–New York–Los Angeles power grid. And he maximizes the internet's potential to make the news cycle timeless and boundless."

In the article, Ciolli described Matt typing away at home 24-7 in his boxer shorts while reading the six hundred to eight hundred "electronic messages" that arrived daily, all while monitoring three television screens and "the electronic sites of twenty major newspapers."

Matt told Ciolli that the independence of his internet website gave him a huge advantage over the larger media establishment because "the advertisers can't do anything to you, and Michael Eisner [then the chairman and CEO of Disney] can't do anything to you."

Matt claimed that without a conventional deadline he could be more selective with his story selection, telling Ciolli, "I don't have to put in the dry filler stuff you see in other columns just to get it done on time."

This is not just another gossip column that happens to be online. My energy goes into the truthful news that is about to be reported or that has been spiked."

The article continued, "Drudge's style is irreverent but not quite cynical. His report has an anarchistic vibe that appeals to those weary of institutions, particularly the media and entertainment conglomerate that hardwire the culture."

"It's a mission of love. As long as the food and rent are paid, I am pretty much where I want to be," Matt told the reporter. "I have the speed on my side and the contact on my side, but I don't know what it can grow into . . . I think I can wake up one day and have a half-million readers and still be totally independent."

The article was also notable for introducing a new name into the public ether, quoting a freelance writer named Andrew Breitbart who "was so impressed with Drudge that he volunteered to help him polish his material."

The article first appeared in *Newsday* on October 1, 1996, and was then syndicated around the country through the Los Angeles Times–Washington Post News Service and caught the eye of television executives. Matt was flown to New York for a meeting with executives, but he would tell friends that nothing came of it.

In November Matt told a reporter for the website Media & Law, "The news comes at me, but I can't predict when . . . That's why I give myself the ability to file when I want rather than every day or at a certain time. Technology lets me be independent. I've got no budget, no bosses, no deadline."

On March 24, 1997, *Los Angeles Times* writer Jerry Lazar met with Matt for an interview. Lazar was covering the "cyberbeat" when he first heard of Matt Drudge, and his interest was piqued.

"The internet seemed boring at the time. But the people on the internet were fascinating," reflects Lazar, who said his perception of Matt at the time was "as an internet guy, not a right-wing guy."

Lazar took the elevator up to the ninth floor to Matt's apartment. "It was a really shitty old bachelor pad apartment in a bad neighborhood. If you looked out the window you could see Capitol Records and the CNN building. A single-guy kind of place that was minimally furnished. There were two computers and a phone and a few other electronics. That was just about it."

Matt came across as "engaging, bright, aware, and driven by this need to get the story out," according to Lazar, who took notes as Matt explained how he was able to get ahead of the news by taking advantage of time zones. "He would go online and discover what was happening in Europe and then post it online in America. It seems so easy now, but at the time he was the only one doing it."

Lazar remembers how in 1997 there was still a public fascination with the concept of the internet. "At that point, most people didn't know what a website was and it was difficult to explain to people that the words on my screen could be seen by people all around the world. It seemed like magic."

"Matt Drudge represented the potential of the internet. He was this guy with no education who had created this space for himself online by rifling through garbage cans, literally. It was a great story."

After the interview the two took a walk together down Cahuenga, stopping at a 24-7 newsstand where Matt "loaded up on newspapers" before walking back to the apartment.

Lazar observes, "He didn't seem at all guarded. We had negotiated ahead of time to leave his address out of the article, which wasn't unusual. He was forthcoming and straightforward. The only exception came when I asked him about his job at CBS. I asked him for names of other people to talk to, and he came up with all kinds of reasons why he didn't know a single person from all those years he said he had worked at the gift shop. That was strange."

At one point during the interview, Matt saw a story he liked on one of his screens and jumped up out of his chair in excitement, "hopping around the room like a kangaroo."

"It was childlike and seemed at odds with his otherwise composed self," says Lazar.

Matt gave Lazar Andrew Breitbart's number for a quote. "The impression I got from Matt was that Andrew was a flunky. Just some guy who helped out."

The article appeared in the *Los Angeles Times* on March 24, 1997. Lazar wrote, "His email newsletter, the Drudge Report, is mandatory reading for the muckiest-mucks in New York, Washington, and Hollywood, dishing the juiciest gossip from the halls of studios, networks, record companies, political chambers and yes, 'traditional' media outlets."

More media followed. In a May 19, 1997, article for the *Washington Post*, Howard Kurtz wrote, "Suddenly, without warning, he is white hot. *Newsweek* and *People* have stopped by for interviews. Wired has signed him for its Web site. Rush Limbaugh has praised him on the radio. Media heavies fussed over him at the White House Correspondents' Association dinner. For an 'awful student' who never bothered with college, 'it's kind of surreal,' says Drudge."

The story of a throwback in a fedora using new technology to advance an old medium made great copy. That summer in an interview with Associated Press "Cyberspace Writer" Elizabeth Weis, Matt challenged her to a battle of dueling keystrokes to see who would be first in uncovering breaking news of an earthquake in Alaska.

Weis wrote that she came in second by about ten seconds, but with the same report. "As the story had only hit the Alaska state broadcast wire, it's clear that Drudge's sources—and access to confidential passwords—are excellent. As is his timing," she wrote.

———

Despite the often-fawning press, warning signs had emerged that this new form of journalism also had its potential drawbacks.

First, although Matt had many hits, he had also missed badly on many stories, including his reports that the movie *Independence Day* would bomb at the box office, that Microsoft was buying Netscape, and his 1996 prediction that Hillary Clinton would be indicted.

Despite the misses, Matt's reach continued its upward trajectory. Less than two months after ending his relationship with Wired.com, Matt announced on July 16, 1997, that he had struck a deal with the internet's biggest entity, America Online (AOL). It would mean that for the first time since his days at CBS he would be collecting a regular paycheck: $3,000 a month.

Bob Pittman, CEO of the AOL subsidiary America Online Networks, said in a release, "Matt Drudge and AOL share the same ingredients: instant, edgy information . . . and that enables them to be among the very few standouts in cyberspace."

Matt added, "With the Drudge Report, I report on the goings-on in all the media companies in Hollywood without worrying about the backlash of corporate sponsors . . . At AOL, an unorthodox service I'm thrilled to join, that won't change . . . in fact, I may pick up a new source or two."

While the money may have been small, the internet giant was now introducing Matt's site to an even wider audience, increasing both his visibility and his readership.

As Matt Drudge's page views began to swell, so did his social circle. Through Breitbart he had met Arianna Huffington, whom he dubbed "queen of the GOP," and her husband, Michael, who was then a congressman. He had befriended Jeffrey Wells after the columnist reached out to do a profile on the internet maverick for *People* magazine.

"He was appreciative of the attention and the exposure that comes from *People* magazine. Our friendship took off from there," says Wells.

It was Matt's counterculture nature that attracted the writer. "It seemed wonderful what Matt was doing. He wasn't really an essayist or a guy who wrote 1,000-word pieces. It seemed like a window. An opportunity. That was the key that opened everything up. That was the freedom element."

The two attended movie screenings together. In one instance, Wells took Matt as his guest to an afternoon screening of the movie *Titanic*. The two walked out of the theater emotionally affected. "We ran into a publicist in the lobby and I was welling over. We both went out and there was a driving rain in the parking lot. We just sat in the car. We were both in total tears," remembers Wells.

Through Wells, Matt was introduced to movie producer Julia Phillips. "A voice just told me that they would probably hit it off. That they would like each other, enjoy each other's candor."

Wells was right, and the two would become close friends. In Phillips, Matt discovered a powerful, enigmatic personality. In 1973 Phillips made Hollywood history as the first female producer to win an Academy Award for Best Picture for *The Sting*. But her 1990 autobiography *You'll Never Eat Lunch in This Town Again*, which included harsh criticism of friends in high places, alienated key players among the industry's elite, and many in Hollywood never spoke to her again.

On June 26, 1997, Matt's circle expanded even more when right-wing writer David Brock and conservative pundit Laura Ingraham cohosted a dinner party at Brock's Georgetown home and invited him as the featured guest.

It was a who's who of media elites: Andrew Sullivan, Ruth Shalit, and Jeffrey Rosen from the *New Republic*; Bill Press from CNN's *Crossfire*; Howard Fineman from *Newsweek*; Tucker Carlson from the *Weekly Standard*; James Warren of the *Chicago Tribune*; journalist Elizabeth Drew; Republican congressman Mark Foley; and conservative lawyer George Conway.

But Matt would find his closest connections in Ingraham and Brock. Ingraham, who had become a celebrity when she graced the cover of a 1995 *New York Times Magazine* piece on young conservatives, had met Matt at the White House Correspondents' Association spring awards dinner. Brock had made his name as a conservative attack dog and had become a cultlike figure on the right for his takedown of Clarence Thomas's accuser in the 1993 book *The Real Anita Hill*.

"They were like the three amigos for a while," a mutual acquaintance remembers. "For a while they would be seen everywhere together."

For everyone else, Matt had become a point of curiosity as the renegade newcomer. They had all read his work, but now they needed to know: Who was Matt Drudge? However, not everyone was in awe of the new internet reporter.

During the party, Matt approached Howard Fineman and mentioned that he wanted to meet *Newsweek*'s ace investigative reporter

Michael Isikoff. Matt had followed Isikoff's career closely, and they both had a mutual point of interest: President Bill Clinton.

No one had broken more stories on the myriad scandals surrounding the Clinton administration and old real estate dealings known as "Whitewater" than Isikoff. The political right had been all in on what they perceived was the inevitable impeachment of President Clinton through a litany of scandals, and Isikoff was viewed by conservatives as one of a small handful of mainstream journalists who weren't biased by the liberal Beltway orthodoxy.

Fineman suggested to Matt that he show up at the office one day, not thinking Matt would take him up on the offer. Matt showed up at *Newsweek* headquarters the next day asking to speak to Isikoff.

The two talked in the hallway outside the newsroom, where Isikoff let it slip that he was working on a story about the Whitewater investigation and how independent counsel Ken Starr was about to come out with his report on the death of Vince Foster. The words had barely escaped Isikoff's lips when he realized he had made a mistake. He reminded the blogger that he couldn't go public with the not-yet-public bit of information, but Matt was already on his way out the door.

Hours later, one of Isikoff's colleagues uttered the words he had been fearing: "You better check Drudge." There, under a flashing red siren above the Drudge Report banner, read the words "Foster Report Imminent!" The story went on to say that "*Newsweek*'s Isikoff" would report in the magazine's issue due out that Monday that there would be new information about the events that led to the White House lawyer's death.

Isikoff was furious. He hadn't planned on reporting the tidbit yet, not thinking it was newsworthy. But now, thanks to Matt's report, he found himself forced to include a line in his *Newsweek* story.

Later that same week, Matt left a message for Isikoff asking him to return his call. Isikoff said he called back with the intention of letting Matt know "what a sleazebag he was for stealing other reporters' stories."

"I'm surprised you called me back," said Matt.

"I probably shouldn't have," Isikoff shot back.

Matt explained he was working on a story about another woman who was harassed by Clinton.

"Where are you hearing this? What were you told?" asked Isikoff.

"Well, I guess there must be something to this," Matt responded.

Isikoff felt a sense of dread take over.

Matt was on a roll. He had been the subject of fawning media reports, he now had a consistent stream of revenue, his website was growing faster than he ever could have imagined, and he had become the toast of the young conservative movement. But rumors were beginning to emerge over his unorthodox personal behavior.

In July 1997 Matt stopped by Brock's house to celebrate his thirty-fifth birthday holding a bouquet of yellow roses. "Jesus, I thought, Drudge thinks we're going on a date," Brock would later write of the incident in *Blinded by the Right*, which detailed his departure from the conservative movement.

Brock's account continued, "After dinner at the famed West Hollywood restaurant Dan Tana's, he suggested we go bar hopping along the gay strip on Santa Monica Boulevard, which Drudge navigated like a pro. At a bar called Rage I accepted his invitation to dance, but I was much more interested in checking out two guys who were dancing nearby. When the couple disappeared, I asked Drudge if he had seen where the pair had gone. 'Yeah,' Drudge quacked, 'I saw what was going on and I stepped on one of their feet really hard to get rid of them.' The gesture was sweet, in a way, but also scary, and I quickly called it a night."

Brock claimed he soon received an email saying, "Laura [Ingraham] spreading stuff about you and me being fuck buddies. I should be so lucky." Brock decided it was time to unceremoniously end his relationship with Matt.

"Fuck it," Matt told a friend. "He's yesterday's news."

14

BLUMENTHAL VS. DRUDGE

Subject: DRUDGE REPORT FINAL 8/11/97
Date: Sun, 10 Aug 1997 21:09:25 -0700 (PDT)
From: DRUDGE REPORT <drudge@drudgereport.com>
To: drudge@drudgereport.com

XXXXX DRUDGE REPORT FINAL XXXXX AUGUST 11, 1997 XXXXX

GOP: THE BLUMENTHAL OPTION?

Exclusive

The DRUDGE REPORT has learned that top GOP operatives who feel there is a double-standard of only reporting republican shame believe they are holding an ace card: New White House recruit Sidney Blumenthal has a spousal abuse past that has been effectively covered up.

The accusations are explosive.

"There are court records of Blumenthal's violence against his wife," one influential republican, who demanded anonymity, tells the DRUDGE REPORT.

One White House source, also requesting anonymity, says the Blumenthal wife-beating allegation is pure fiction that has been created by Clinton enemies. "[The First Lady] would not have brought him in if he had this in his background," assures the well-placed staffer. "This story about Blumenthal has been in circulation for years."

Last month President Clinton named Sidney Blumenthal an Assistant to the President as part of the Communications Team. He's been brought in to work on communications strategy, special projects, themeing—a newly created position.

Every attempt to reach Blumenthal proved unsuccessful.

The report found its way that night to a computer in Sidney Blumenthal's house. The reaction was immediate. Blumenthal's lawyers sent a tersely worded letter demanding a retraction. The letter read in part, "Your action in disseminating these outrageous falsehoods across the country was despicable. You acted with actual malice in that you knew that these allegations were false but published them anyway. You took no step to verify your allegations . . ."

Two days later, Matt issued a short statement:

I am issuing a retraction of my information regarding Sidney Blumenthal that appeared in the DRUDGE REPORT on August 11, 1997.

Matt Drudge

But the damage was done. Blumenthal's lawyers were going full-speed ahead, issuing subpoenas to anyone who might be connected to Matt, no matter how loosely.

Longtime conservative operative Barbara Ledeen couldn't believe her eyes when the man showed up at her door with an order for her to appear in court as a witness in a lawsuit between Sidney Blumenthal and Matt Drudge.

"I didn't know Matt Drudge," said Ledeen. "But I knew enough to know that we needed help."

Ledeen and her husband, author Michael Ledeen, may have never met Matt, but they had more than enough experience with Blumenthal, whom they described as "vicious" and "vindictive" for his attacks on their conservative advocacy work. After receiving the subpoena at their home asking them to turn over "all kinds of information," Leeden called her friend, libertarian activist David Horowitz.

"You have to help Matt Drudge," she said to Horowitz.

Horowitz, who had founded the libertarian Individual Rights Foundation, had never met Matt, either, but after being contacted by Ledeen, Horowitz believed it was a noble cause. Horowitz agreed to allow his foundation, which mainly fought speech codes on college campuses, to represent Matt's defense.

Horowitz remembered, "Matt and I had breakfast. At the time I don't think he realized or appreciated the real danger he was in with this lawsuit. The goal was to destroy Drudge, and even if Blumenthal knew he couldn't win the case, he could easily drain Drudge dry."

"He grudgingly accepted our help," added Horowitz.

With Matt's permission, Horowitz went to work creating a defense fund, which raised money through direct mail and internet appeals to pay the lawyers' fees. He then set up a meeting with Matt and Individual Rights Foundation lawyers Manny Klausner and Patrick Manshardt. Manshardt was excited to take the case, seeing Matt Drudge, and all the Drudge Report represented, as important for the future of internet freedom.

"Matt Drudge didn't have the resources at the time to respond to that kind of thing," says Manshardt. "I took this case because I believed it was in the public interest. Matt Drudge was a private citizen and Blumenthal, who was this high-ranking government official, was going at him."

From the beginning, Matt's defense never believed Blumenthal had a legitimate case. "To prove defamation there is a very high standard to meet. Matt Drudge actually reported that there were rumors, which was true. It was a rumor. To make the case, Blumenthal would have had to prove that he knew what he had reported was not true and had done so with malice," explains Manshardt. "Legally, we felt we had Blumenthal over the barrel."

Blumenthal also incorrectly believed the source of the rumor to be the *Wall Street Journal*'s John Fund. According to Manshardt, Matt hadn't even met Fund at that point.

Manshardt believed the real reason for the lawsuit had little to do with Matt Drudge; rather, the Drudge Report was being used as a vehicle for Blumenthal to unravel what he perceived as a right-wing conspiracy.

"At the time Drudge and David Brock and Laura Ingraham were stuck at the hip. Syd [Blumenthal] saw this and really believed there was this conspiracy and wanted insight. That was the primary reason they were doing this," says Manshardt. "We liked to joke that I ran the L.A. office of the right-wing conspiracy, and that there was no vast right-wing conspiracy, but a very narrow and focused one."

Ledeen, who had founded the Independent Women's Forum as a counterpunch to the feminist progressive movements of the 1990s, also believed that the real goal of the lawsuit was to attack the conservative movement: "We had long been on President Clinton's enemy list. Blumenthal already had an iron in the fire. This lawsuit was him taking it out and trying to use it."

In an interview, Matt concurred, adding that it was his growing influence that had made him a target of Blumenthal:

The reason I'm attacked is that I'm being heard. Powerful people are reading me. What I say is getting picked up. So the focus is on me. I'm the first one out and I have a big audience. Radio was licensed by government, television was licensed by government. But the internet was built by government and isn't licensed by anyone. The Net is a lot like the pamphlets of the old days, and I'm like a pamphleteer speaking my mind. But now the audience is the world.

In the subpoenas, Blumenthal's lawyers requested "any and all documents" relating to Blumenthal, Matt Drudge, former ambassador Richard Carlson and his son, *Weekly Standard* writer Tucker Carlson, former *American Spectator* writer David Brock, and Barbara and Michael Ledeen.

It was not only Matt's career that was at stake; the case also had major implications for the First Amendment and the future of internet news. In the court filing, Blumenthal argued that because Matt didn't have a physical paper, he was not a reporter, and as a result, was not entitled to the protected status that the law affords journalists.

"Blumenthal tried to make the case that he was just some guy with a computer in a shitty Hollywood apartment," reflects Manshardt. "We all knew at the time that if the court decided that the First Amendment didn't protect you unless you were part of a major news organization it would have had a chilling effect on freedom."

———

Blumenthal may have been correct in his belief that there were separate factions plotting to take down the Clinton presidency, but he was looking mostly in the wrong places. Most of Clinton's threats from the right didn't match those on his subpoena list. They were gathered on the other side of the country.

While Matt was on the West Coast, on the East Coast conservative attorneys Ann Coulter, Kellyanne Fitzpatrick, Laura Ingraham, and New York tobacco lawyer George Conway III were plotting how to leverage President Clinton's ongoing litigation with Paula Jones against him.

George Conway had first gotten involved after seeing a report in the *New York Times* that the White House was floating the idea of making a presidential immunity argument in the Paula Jones case.

"The argument would be that because the president was president, he could not be sued while in office for the stuff that happened before he was president. And I just thought that was crazy, that doesn't make any sense," said Conway.

Coulter would take it a step further, saying in an interview, "We were terrified that Jones would settle. It was contrary to our purpose of bringing down the president."

Conway wrote an op-ed, published in the *Los Angeles Times*, arguing that no man is above the law. The article caught the attention of Paula Jones's lawyer, Jerome Marcus, who brought Conway in to begin writing legal briefs to assist in their battle against Clinton.

In the summer of 1997 Conway was introduced to Matt Drudge by Ingraham. Conway would prove a valuable source. It was reportedly Conway who called Matt to feed him the details of a woman named Kathleen Willey, a former White House volunteer aide who alleged that Bill Clinton had sexually assaulted her on November 29, 1993.

Matt wrote out the holiday "EXCLUSIVE" titled "ants in the picnic basket."

Coming just hours after the President "adamantly" denies harassing Paula Jones, the DRUDGE REPORT has learned that NEWSWEEK ace investigative reporter Michael Isikoff is hot on the trail of a new development that threatens to ignite premature holiday fireworks at the White House. Reports have surfaced that Isikoff has been in contact with a former White House staffer who may offer "pattern" evidence of improper sexual conduct on the part of the President.

At this hour it is unclear whether Isikoff will pull the pieces of this explosive story together before deadline.

Other reporters may also be on the trail of this new development.

The story is said to involve a federal employee sexually propositioned by the President on federal property.

If true, the new account would be markedly different from the Jones' scenario, which involved pre-presidential actions long ago and far away.

On October 8, 1997, Conway reportedly emailed Matt again, introducing himself as "a friend of Laura" with an "exclusive" about Paula Jones's claim (which was later dropped) that the "distinguishing characteristic" of the president's anatomy was a curvature caused by a malady known as Peyronie's disease.

"Disgusting or what????" Conway reportedly exclaimed in the email.

Matt published the rumor, but these two posts would only serve as appetizers for what was to come next. Tapes were floating around that had been created by a White House civil servant named Linda Tripp. Tripp had met a young White House intern, Monica Lewinsky, who said she had been having an affair with the president. As the relationship began to unravel, Lewinsky was becoming increasingly unhinged. Tripp explained the situation to her literary agent, Lucianne Goldberg, who suggested she begin taping the conversations.

"She didn't like the idea of taping her friend. But I told her, if you don't have proof, these people are going to eat that poor girl alive," says Goldberg.

Goldberg shared the news with her friend Ann Coulter, who suggested they bring attorney Jim Moody into the fold. Coulter had met Moody during an internship at the Department of Justice. Moody was an MIT graduate who helped design the cruise missile system, and the two had spent time attending Grateful Dead concerts across the country.

Tripp personally delivered the tapes she secretly recorded to Moody on January 9, 1998. Tripp's instructions were clear. No copies were to be made. The tapes needed to be preserved and handed off to the investigators.

"I didn't want a circus," recalls Tripp. "My only goal was to get these tapes into the hands of the investigators. And as quickly as possible."

Moody, who is legally blind, agreed.

George Conway arrived at Moody's office a few days later, where he discovered the lawyer struggling to get the tapes to play in an old Dictaphone: "He's fumbling with the buttons. And I'm watching this, and I start getting worried that this blind man is going to erase evidence that could lead to the impeachment of a president."

More people would soon be brought into the loop. Lucianne Goldberg advised Linda Tripp to reach out to Michael Isikoff in late September, asking him if he would be willing to meet at the walk-up condo of Goldberg's son, Jonah. Isikoff showed up at the Manhattan apartment on October 6, where he found Goldberg and Tripp waiting with a tape player in hand. Goldberg told him they had the Lewinsky tapes and suggested that Isikoff listen.

Isikoff politely declined, answering, "As a journalist, it would put me in a bad position to do that."

In point of fact, the seasoned reporter was worried that by listening to part of the tapes he would be inserting himself into the story. Isikoff remembers, "There were pretty strong guidelines that you don't get involved. That is a violation. There were strict guidelines handed down. That was the culture I was raised in. It was a sort of seat of the pants split second. It was pretty clear this was an ongoing process—they were trying to get me to coach them. It appeared to be an effort to make me a part of something that I was ethically obligated to stay out of."

They spent the next hour talking and then gave Isikoff the name of the other woman: Monica Lewinsky. Again, Goldberg insisted he listen to the tapes. Tripp reached for the recorder and pushed the play button.

"Wait," said Isikoff. "I'm not sure I should be doing his. It probably isn't a good idea for me to listen."

Tripp hit stop on the tape player. Whatever was on the tapes, Isikoff told them, he would need more corroboratory documentation if he was going to write an article alleging that the president of the United States was having an affair with an intern. He assured them he would keep working, and then left the apartment.

"He ran out of there," recalls Goldberg. "I think he had a car waiting for him outside to take him to appear on *Hardball*."

Over the next several weeks, Tripp and Goldberg continued to stay in touch with Isikoff, feeding him information and waiting for the story to break. But as the days went by, Goldberg's crew was growing impatient.

Since the first day of his presidency, conservatives had been trying to prove Clinton was corrupt and unfit for office, but every time they thought they had him, the football would be yanked back and they would be left tumbling through the air catching nothing but wind. But this time, they believed it would be different.

The day before Clinton was to give a sworn deposition, Paula Jones's legal team was notified of the tapes and their content. On January 17, 1998, Clinton gave a sworn deposition denying having a "sexual relationship," "sexual affair," or "sexual relations" with Lewinsky.

The president's sworn testimony directly contradicted the information on the tapes. They finally had him, they thought. Now they needed to get the information out. And fast.

On the evening of January 17, Isikoff called Moody and Goldberg to let them know the story wouldn't be running. The editors at *Newsweek* made the decision that the taped conversations amounted to hearsay and were not enough to publish a story that could lead to the impeachment of the president.

"Isikoff was very excited," recalls Goldberg.

For Goldberg, it was more evidence of the leftist media protecting their own. She was determined to make sure the story wouldn't get squashed. A friend suggested she call Matt Drudge.

Matt had been following the Clinton case closely with a member of Goldberg's inner circle having already leaked bits and pieces of the story, but now, for the first time, he was hearing the entire story— along with *Newsweek*'s role.

"I did know Matt Drudge, but I hadn't met him. And I was with friends who trusted him. And there was no other place to go. Isikoff had been fiddling for months. My friends told me, 'Hey, you should call Drudge.' So that is what I did. I picked up the phone, called Matt Drudge, and gave him the story," says Goldberg.

It was shortly before 10:00 p.m., eastern time, when Goldberg picked up the phone to dial Matt in Los Angeles.

In Goldberg's words, "I began to tell Matt the story and he was like a kid in a candy store. Drudge loved it. He was like, 'Oh, boy this is great.'"

Less than an hour later, Goldberg got a call that the story had been posted on the Drudge Report. "I couldn't believe how quickly it went up. I said, 'You watch, this will change journalism forever.'"

PART
2

15

Matt Drudge positioned the mouse, suspending the pointer icon over the Send button of his computer.

This was *his* moment. And he knew it. He was just one click away, but he would have to wait.

Only a few minutes had passed since he sent the copy to his source for review. Now all that was left to do was stare at the screen and wait to hear back for confirmation.

> NEWSWEEK KILLS STORY ON WHITE HOUSE INTERN XXXX
> BLOCKBUSTER REPORT: 23-YEAR-OLD, FORMER WHITE
> HOUSE INTERN, SEX-RELATIONSHIP WITH PRESIDENT!!!

The big question was: Did he *really* want to risk everything? Then? For this?

Only four months had passed since Sidney Blumenthal had filed a $30 million defamation suit against him after posting a story alleging that the Clinton confidant had abused his wife. Maybe, some close to Matt had suggested, it would be best to keep a low profile. Just tone it down a little bit. At least until the case is resolved.

The DRUDGE REPORT has learned that reporter Michael Isikoff developed the story of his career, only to have it spiked by top NEWSWEEK suits hours before publication.

Of course, he knew what was staring back at him on the screen was bigger than his soaring page views, the AOL deal that gave him his first steady paycheck, or even the looming Blumenthal lawsuit.

Larger than any one news cycle.

In Matt's eyes, this was about taking a sledgehammer to the media establishment complex.

A young woman, 23 . . . wrote long love letters to President Clinton, which she delivered through a delivery service.

Those days where a small group of editors and television producers decided for the rest of the country what constituted the news were over. They just didn't know it yet.

At the last minute, at 6pm Saturday evening, NEWSWEEK magazine killed a story that was destined to shake official Washington to its foundation . . .

And now they were trying to do it again. This time it was *Newsweek*, a shining pillar of the journalism community, spiking the story that could lead to the impeachment of President William Jefferson Clinton.

She was a frequent visitor at the White House after midnight, where she checked in the WAVE logs as visiting a secretary named Betty Currie, 57 . . . tapes of intimate phone conversations exist . . .

NEWSWEEK and Isikoff were planning to name the woman. Word of the story's impending release caused blind chaos in media circles; TIME magazine spent Saturday scrambling for its own version of the story. The NEW YORK POST on Sunday was set to front the young intern's affair but . . .

The stakes couldn't be higher. He needed to make sure there were no loose ends. He had tried contacting *Newsweek* but had no luck. Calls to the office went straight to after-hours voicemail.

He called Michael Isikoff, punching the numbers into his landline and waiting.

"Hello," an upbeat female voice answered. It was Isikoff's wife, journalist Lisa Stein.

"Is Mike there?"

"Yes, he is. Whom shall I say is calling?"

"It's Matt Drudge."

"I'm sorry. He's asleep right now and I'm not going to wake him up. Not for you."

Dial tone.

The story was set to break just hours after President Clinton testified in the Paula Jones sexual harassment case . . . Isikoff was not available for comment late Saturday. NEWSWEEK was on voicemail.

An instant message popped up on his screen. It was from his source. She had reviewed the story. It was confirmed.

Spell-check.

Click.

At precisely 9:32 p.m. and two seconds by his L.A. clock, Matt Drudge tapped down on the mouse with his index finger, sending the words on his screen whirling through time and space at the speed of now.

Hurling beams of information out of his small Hollywood apartment through telephone lines.

Crossing states.

Bouncing off satellites, spreading tiny dots of data from coast to coast into living rooms and offices, landing a heartbeat later on a desktop computer at 1600 Pennsylvania Avenue . . . in front of the leader of the free world.

"Well, I had a little anxiety the next day, of course, because of the Drudge Report," Clinton would later testify before the grand jury.

Having published, Matt Drudge sat alone in his Hollywood apartment. He began sobbing. He realized that from that moment forward his life was never going to be the same.

16

AFTERMATH

By the time the sun had risen on the morning of Sunday, January 18, 1998, the story about the president and the intern had become the talk of the Beltway, leaving the news establishment unsure of how to handle what they had seen on the Drudge Report.

Earlier that morning, David Tell, an editorial writer for the *Weekly Standard*, called Michael Isikoff for guidance. "There was a story on the Drudge Report saying that *Newsweek* spiked a story that was about to expose a sexual relationship between Clinton and a young former intern," he recalls. Tell's boss, conservative commentator Bill Kristol, wanted to mention it on the Sunday show *This Week with George Stephanopoulos*.

"What should I tell him [Kristol]?" asked Tell.

Isikoff was seething and would later confess that he had "certain homicidal tendencies" after seeing months of his hard work end up on the renegade web publisher's website, but he summoned up the energy to compose himself enough to answer: "Look, if Kristol wants to go with something based on Drudge, that's his problem . . . How could he rely on anything the guy writes?"

Tell promised to relay the message to Kristol. Kristol, having other sources in *Newsweek*'s newsroom, made the decision to place the story in front of the national television audience during his national television appearance anyway.

"The story in Washington this morning," Kristol told Stephanopoulos, "is that *Newsweek* was going to go with a big story based on tape-recorded conversations in which a woman who was a summer intern at the White House, an intern of Leon Panetta's—"

"And Bill, where did it come from?" a visibly upset Stephanopoulos—who had worked as White House Communications Director in the Clinton White House—interrupted. "The Drudge Report. We've all seen how discredited that's been."

Kristol pushed back. "No. No. No. They had screaming arguments at *Newsweek* magazine yesterday. They finally didn't go with the story. It's going to be a question of whether the media is now going to report what are pretty well-validated charges of presidential behavior in the White House."

Next, Sam Donaldson intervened, suggesting no one comment further until *Newsweek* had a chance to explain their side of the story. *This Week* moved on to the next item, but behind the scenes, editors and newspaper executives raced to match the story that had been broken on the internet by Matt Drudge.

———

And Matt was just getting started. For nearly four days the Drudge Report completely owned the story as Lucianne Goldberg and her friends continued feeding Matt information, which he posted online free of charge for the world to see.

Web Posted: 01/18/98 22:33:48 PST—FORMER WHITE HOUSE INTERN CALLED; NEW BACKGROUND DETAILS EMERGE
World Exclusive
Must Credit the DRUDGE REPORT

The DRUDGE REPORT has learned that former White House intern, Monica Lewinsky, 23, has been subpoenaed to give a deposition in the Paula Jones case.

Web Posted: 01/19/98 14:54:06 PST—FORMER WHITE HOUSE INTERN DENIES SEX WITH PRESIDENT IN SWORN AFFIDAVIT
World Exclusive
Must Credit the DRUDGE REPORT

Former White House intern Monica Lewinsky, 23, has denied having any "sexual relationship with President Clinton" in a sworn affidavit, the DRUDGE REPORT has learned. Lewinsky's sworn written statement was executed last week after she was served with a subpoena in the Paula Jones sexual harassment case.

NBC was busy developing a story Tuesday afternoon on Lewinsky. Through a suspected leak, the network obtained a copy of Lewinsky's affidavit and was reading portions of it to sources to provoke comment.

Web Posted: 01/20/98 19:57:07 PST—CONTROVERSY SWIRLS AROUND TAPES OF FORMER WHITE HOUSE INTERN, AS STARR MOVES IN!
World Exclusive
Must Credit the DRUDGE REPORT

Federal investigators are now in possession of intimate taped conversations of a former White House intern, age

23, discussing details of her alleged sexual relationship with President Clinton, the DRUDGE REPORT has learned.

The tapes were made by a federal employee who has been granted immunity. MORE

According to sources in and out of government, Whitewater independent counsel Kenneth Starr became involved in the situation when he received intelligence that senior administration officials may have offered federal jobs to a young woman in an effort to prevent stories from going public— stories involving sexual episodes that allegedly occurred in a room off the Oval Office.

Web Posted: 01/21/98 11:32:53 PST—~~LEWINSKY NIGHTMARE CONTINUES~~ U.N. AMBASSADOR RICHARDSON OFFERED ME A JOB DURING BREAKFAST MEETING AT WATERGATE HOTEL, SHE SAID; INVESTIGATORS PROBE POSSIBILITY OF CLINTON DNA . . . MOVING SOON ON THE DRUDGE REPORT X X X X

But in terms of gross-out value, the most shocking stories of all were still to come. Goldberg gave Matt a story about a dress that the young intern had saved that had the President's DNA on it. In Goldberg's words, "I knew it was going to explode, but I didn't think it was going to explode like it did."

Web Posted: 01/21/98 12:56:27 PST—WATERGATE 1998

WORLD EXCLUSIVE
MUST CREDIT THE DRUDGE REPORT
CONTAINS GRAPHIC DESCRIPTIONS

REPORT: LEWINSKY OFFERED U.N. JOB; INVESTIGATORS: DNA TRAIL MAY EXIST

U.N. AMBASSADOR RICHARDSON OFFERED ME A JOB DURING A BREAKFAST MEETING AT THE WATERGATE HOTEL—WORDS WHITE HOUSE INTERN MONICA LEW-INSKY, 24, ALLEGEDLY TOLD PENTAGON WORKER LINDA TRIPP LATE IN DECEMBER 1997.

THE OFFER CAME AS LEWINSKY WAS ASKING TO RETURN TO THE WHITE HOUSE, THE DRUDGE REPORT HAS LEARNED, UNHAPPY IN THE PENTAGON JOB SHE HELD—A JOB THAT SHE STARTED IN APRIL 1996 AFTER BEING RELEASED FROM A WHITE HOUSE POSITION.

"THEY WANTED HER OUT OF THE WHITE HOUSE DURING THE ELECTION," A SOURCE CLOSE TO THE INVESTIGATION TELLS THE DRUDGE REPORT.

AMBASSADOR RICHARDSON WAS NOT AVAILABLE FOR COMMENT.

WHITE HOUSE PRESS SECRETARY MIKE MCCURRY OFFERED NOTHING WHEN ASKED ABOUT THE ALLEGED RICHARDSON JOB OFFER DURING WEDNESDAY'S PRESS BRIEFING.

SEPARATELY, THE DRUDGE REPORT HAS LEARNED, INVES-TIGATORS HAVE BECOME CONVINCED THAT THERE MAY BE A DNA TRAIL THAT COULD CONFIRM PRESIDENT CLIN-TON'S SEXUAL INVOLVEMENT WITH LEWINSKY, A RELA-TIONSHIP THAT WAS CAPTURED IN LEWINSKY'S OWN VOICE ON AUDIO TAPE.

TRIPP HAS SHARED WITH INVESTIGATORS A CONVER-SATION WHERE LEWINSKY ALLEGEDLY CONFIDED THAT SHE KEPT A GARMENT WITH CLINTON'S DRIED SEMEN ON IT—A GARMENT SHE SAID SHE WOULD NEVER WASH!

"All original reporting, not from *Newsweek*," Matt later boasted.

On January 25, 1998, Tim Russert put Matt on his *Meet the Press* panel alongside *New York Times* columnist William Safire, *Newsweek*'s Michael Isikoff, and *National Journal*'s Stuart Taylor.

Afterward, Matt fielded questions from reporters who had gathered outside NBC Studios. Asked if he was going to back off for a few days from releasing more stories with Clinton's State of the Union Address coming up, Matt answered, "That's up to you guys. I'm not backing off . . . I'm just one man reporting what I see and I intend no mercy. I'm going to get to the bottom of this and I'm working on it hard."

In an interview with David Sheff that appeared in the June 1998 issue of *Playboy*, Matt hit back against the charge that he owed his newfound fame to nothing more than an uncanny ability to steal others' stories. He told Sheff, "New inventions come along and knock down old inventions. And again, my Lewinsky story was original. To report that *Newsweek* killed the story is original reporting. No one in the mainstream press has given me credit for that."

He cataloged several original stories he ran, including the dress, and then continued, "That's a lot of work, a lot of original reporting on a serious story. So how can they maintain I'm just stealing other people's stories?"

Pressed in the interview on journalistic ethics and standards, Matt rejected the idea that reporters should be objective. "You don't get a license to report. You get a license to style hair. Since World War II, we've had an era in which journalism is supposed to be objective. That's crap. That's a new phenomenon. The earlier press had nothing to do with objectivity. This whole objectivity thing is a fraud."

Matt would soon take the public discourse into uncharted territory when on August 22, 1998, he reported the following:

In a bizarre daytime sex session, that occurred just off the Oval Office in the White House, President Clinton watched as intern Monica Lewinsky allegedly masturbated with his cigar.

It has been learned that several major news organizations have confirmed the shocking episode and are now struggling to find ways to report the full Monica Lewinsky/Bill Clinton grossout.

Media Bigfeet are trying to reconstruct one sex session that reportedly took place as Yasser Arafat waited in the Rose Garden for his scheduled meeting with the president!

The story put newscasts in an unprecedented situation. *Washington Times* editor in chief Wesley Pruden would later write of the dilemma facing editors in a column for the *Washington Times*, "Some of the answers that Monica gave the grand jury, and the questions the president didn't want to answer, have not been reported only because editors of newspapers . . . haven't figured out how to describe them without offending pimps and pornographers."

Goldberg states, "It had people very upset . . . It was almost a contest. People were dying to get the story out but didn't know how to do it. Matt didn't have that problem. He didn't have editors or censors. He was free to post what he wanted."

The series of exclusive banner headlines peppering the Drudge Report launched a nationwide debate over what constituted journalism, with most of the establishment media eager to circle the wagons.

After the January 25 *Meet the Press* broadcast, Russert and NBC News president Andy Lack received a letter from Sidney Blumenthal's attorney, William McDaniel: "You introduced Mr. Drudge as offering 'expert insight and analysis' when you introduced him on *Meet the Press*, and you then offered Mr. Drudge to your audience as though you believed him to be a reputable journalist. The Blu-menthals are interested in learning whether you intend to testify on behalf of Mr. Drudge . . . to vouch for his credentials as a journalist. If you do, we wish to take your deposition."

Russert reportedly responded by calling McDaniel personally, telling him, "I don't vouch for anyone."

In his introduction on NBC's *Today*, Matt Lauer called the Drudge Report "a media gossip page known for below-the-beltway reporting."

"I've heard calling it a report is too generous," quipped White House press secretary Mike McCurry.

In *Time* Michael Kinsley wrote that the Lewinsky story broken by Drudge "is for the internet what the Kennedy assassination was to TV news."

The first lady even warned the public during a February press conference of the dangers of the internet when asked about the net's role in the dissemination of news:

> As exciting as these new developments are . . . there are a
> number of serious issues without any kind of editing function
> or gate-keeping function. What does it mean to have the right
> to defend your reputation, or to respond to what someone
> says? There used to be this old saying that the lie can be
> halfway around the world before the truth gets its boots on.
> Well, today, the lie can be twice around the world before the
> truth gets out of bed to find its boots. I mean, it is just beyond
> imagination what can be disseminated.

Further, when asked whether she favored regulation of the net, the first lady left the door open: "Anytime an individual or an institu-tion or an invention leaps so far out ahead of that balance and throws a system, whatever it might be—political, economic, technological—out of balance, you've got a problem, because then it can lead to the oppression of people's rights, it can lead to the manipulation of information, it can lead to all kinds of bad outcomes which we have seen historically. So we're going to have to deal with that."

President Bill Clinton was reportedly much more concise, coining a nickname for the web aggregator—Sludge.

————

In the months that followed, the historic weight of what he had done set in on Matt. He began to believe that he was in danger and that something nefarious could happen to him. If ever the Clinton deep state, which he had spent years obsessing over, had a reason to spring to life—this was it.

Was he being followed? At times he believed he was.

Had his computer been hacked? He didn't think so—but he told friends that he was sure someone had tried.

Maybe, he thought, the police would come barging into his Hollywood apartment with a warrant for his arrest for some trumped-up charges? He told friends he worried that one day he would arrive at his car to find it surrounded by police after someone had planted a bag of cocaine in the trunk.

His attorney Patrick Manshardt remembers, "Drudge seemed more worried that the powers that be would do something terrible to him—arrest him, eliminate him, frame him. That seemed to be his concern. He was concerned there was some sort of deep state action that would be used against him. He was serious."

17

THE SPEECH

Doug Harbrecht had no idea what he was about to get himself into. "I noticed that everybody had bad things to say about Matt Drudge, but meanwhile everyone was checking out his site all the time," according to Harbrecht.

"Someone suggested, Why don't we have him come to the National Press Club? I thought it was a great idea. We all knew something was happening with the internet and news, but what exactly that was remained unclear. I invited him, but boy did I upset a lot of journalists."

The vast majority of established journalists had been lambasting Matt. Harbrecht, who served as president of the highly respected National Press Club, wanted to give him the opportunity to make his case, while allowing other journalists to question and confront the web publisher on his news-gathering methods: "The way I was thinking about it, this guy is a big newsmaker and these are newsmaker lunches. So I went ahead with it. I thought I knew what was happening. I thought I knew what I was getting into. But this became big, a lot bigger, than I imagined it could ever be."

It was exactly the opportunity Matt had been waiting for. Representatives of the major media players would all be there. The speech and the Q&A that followed was going to be televised live on C-SPAN, and then replayed at later dates. He relished being given the platform to make the case for the populist movement in media he had long envisioned. Every word in the speech would be carefully crafted.

Matt arrived at the Press Club with his friend Ann Coulter at his side. The two took their seats and sat quietly as Harbrecht introduced him.

"My reaction to having our speaker today at the National Press Club was the same as a lot of other members," Harbrecht told the room full of journalists on the afternoon of June 2, 1998. "Why do we want to give a forum to that guy?"

Those assembled were waiting for a show. Countless more were tuning in to C-SPAN to see, for the first time, the face that had pioneered this new form of media that had rocked the country. Matt stepped up to the podium and nervously scanned the audience. He began, "Applause for Matt Drudge in Washington at the Press Club. Now there's a scandal. It's the kind of thing I'd have a headline for."

Nervous laughter filled the room. Matt picked up his fedora, planted it firmly on his head, and then began to speak about his unlikely rise:

I used to walk these streets as an aimless teen, young adult; walk by ABC News over on DeSales, daydream; stare up at the *Washington Post* newsroom over on 15th Street; look up longingly, knowing I'd never get in—didn't go to the right schools, never enjoyed any school, as a matter of fact, didn't come from a well-known family—nor was I even remotely connected to a powerful publishing dynasty.

Matt paused to fiddle with his fedora, affixing it tighter to his head. His voice began to rise as he launched into a philosophical treatise on the unprecedented information revolution this new technology of the internet was about to launch and the resulting democratization of the news that he was confident would follow.

There is a hunger for unedited information, absent corporate considerations. As the first guy who has made a name for himself on the internet, I've been invited to more and more high-toned gatherings such as this, the last being a conference on Internet & Society and some word I couldn't pronounce, up at Harvard a week ago. And I mention this not just to blow my own horn, but to make a point. Exalted minds—the panelists' and the audience's average IQ exceeds the Dow Jones—didn't appear to have a clue what this internet's going to do; what we're going to make of it, what we're going to—what this is all going to turn into. But I have glimpses.

The internet would be the great equalizer, he continued, giving voice to anyone with a connection to the information superhighway.

We have entered an era vibrating with the din of small voices. Every citizen can be a reporter, can take on the powers that be. The difference between the internet, television and radio, magazines, newspapers is the two-way communication. The net gives as much voice to a thirteen-year-old computer geek like me as to a CEO or Speaker of the House. We all become equal. And you would be amazed what the ordinary guy knows.

From a little corner in my Hollywood apartment, in the company of nothing more than my 486 computer and my six—six-toed cat, I have consistently been able to break big stories, thanks to this network of ordinary guys.

And this is something new. This marks the first time that an individual has access to the newswires outside of a newsroom. You get to read all the news from the Associated Press, UPI, Reuters, to the more—the more arcane Agence France-Presse and the Chenois. I'm a personal fan of the Chenois Press.

And there was a time when only newsrooms had access to the full pictures of the day's events. But now any citizen does. We get to see the kinds of cuts that are made for all kinds of reasons—endless layers of editors with endless agendas changing bits and pieces, so by the time the newspaper hits your welcome mat it had no meaning. Now, with a modem, anyone can follow the world and report on the world—no middle man, no Big Brother. And I guess this changes everything.

Fears over the new technology had several historical parallels, he continued, but in time the internet and the news industry wouldn't just coexist but become codependent.

When radio lost out to television, there was anxiety. The people in the radio business were absolutely anxious and demanded government stop the upcoming television wave. Television was very nervous about other mediums coming forward—cable. The movies were—didn't want sitcoms to be taped at movie studios for fear it would take away from the movies. No, television saved the movies. The internet is going to save the news business. I envision a future where there'll be three hundred million reporters, where anyone from anywhere can report for any reason. It's freedom of participation, absolutely realized.

Matt concluded his speech by making the case that protecting the freedom of the internet was vital to preserving American democracy.

Our Republic and its press will rise or fall together. An able, disinterested, public-spirited press . . . can preserve that public virtue without which popular government is a sham and a mockery . . . The power to mold the future of the republic will be in the hands of the journalists of the future generations. And if Pulitzer were alive today in this time, he would add "using future mediums."

I was walking the streets of Washington—the streets I grew up in—last night. Found myself in front of the *Washington Post* building again, looking up, this time not longingly. This time I laughed. Let the future begin.

———

Matt looked up, scanning faces for reactions. The room was charged. "You could feel the electricity," Harbrecht remembers.

Still at the podium, Matt began taking questions submitted by the journalists in the room and read by Harbrecht. "I was trying to question him as if he were a rookie or a cub reporter," says Harbrecht. "He couldn't have been more prepared."

Q: What is the biggest mistake you have made so far?

Matt: That's a really good question. I've made a few mistakes. Ever doubting my ability was my biggest mistake, because in the beginning I didn't think much that I had the right to report things. But I was wrong. Boy, was I wrong. Whenever I tend to think, you know, "Oh, I probably shouldn't be reporting on the president of the United States, respect the office." I respect the office so much I want to cover it. And you know I maintain who is telling more truth this summer, me or the president of the United States? So I don't have many regrets. I don't have many regrets. I don't have many regrets in that area, except for doubting that this was my God-given right and as an American citizen, and embracing it, and saying liberty is just wonderful, thanks to the people who have come before me who have stood up for it.

Q: Do you see your methods and your medium as controversial in and of themselves, or are they contributing to the degradation of serious or hard traditional journalism?

Matt: Well, you know, the editor of *Civilization* magazine, Adam Goodheart, wrote a great op-ed in the *New York Times* talking about, "Is this really something new, this type of fast reporting . . ." He maintains it was a going back to our foundations when the press was founded, in quite a different atmosphere, when the press would report that the president's mother was a common prostitute brought over by the British army. Imagine if someone did that now. We have a great tradition of freedom of the press in this country, unpopular press. If the first lady is concerned about this internet cycle, what would she have done during the heyday when there was twelve, thirteen editions of a paper in one day? What would she have done with that news cycle? That's the foundation. That's what makes this club great . . . the tradition. And I think we have a tradition of provocative press. And I maintain that I'm the new face of that. I'll take that for a season.

Q: How much do you embroider or make up in your online items?

Matt: Everything I print from my apartment, everything I publish, I believe to be true and accurate. I put my name on every single thing I write. No "periscope" here. No "Washington Whispers" here. I put my name [on] it; I'll answer to anything I write. I'll make mistakes. I'll retract them if I have to, apologize for it, try to make it right. But as I've pointed out, the main organizations in this country have let us down every once in a while and end up in trouble with editors. So I don't maintain that an editor is salvation. There won't be editors in the future with the internet world, with citizen reporting just by the nature of it. That doesn't scare me. There's a notion that sticks and stones may break my bones, but words will kill me. I don't believe it. I get maligned every day on the news groups. I'm still standing. I still have a smile on my face.

After the speech and Q&A had concluded, Harbrecht retreated to his upstairs office where he quickly discovered how the public had felt about his job performance.

"It immediately began," recalls Harbrecht, who for the first time had found himself being labeled unfair and biased for his treatment of Matt. "We started getting emails from all over the country. That was when I found out what the meaning of the word 'troll' was. I got slammed, right down to my aunt and uncle. Rush Limbaugh spent time on his radio show laying into me. I would prove a perfect elitist foil."

"Matt Drudge's speech became the most commented event that the Press Club had ever had, but it wasn't until five years later that I read that speech and realized how brilliant it was," Harbrecht adds.

As members of the news media slowly filtered out of the room, they were accompanied by a cascade of murmurs and sly grins. These were men and women with journalism degrees from some of the most prestigious schools in the country and working for some of the most hallowed media institutions in the world. For generations, they had built their reputation as guardians of information who sought accountability from the powerful, and in their eyes, had more than proved their worth several times over. From Watergate, to the Pentagon Papers, to the Iran–Contra affair, they took their oath to uphold the public trust as sacrosanct.

Now, in a single speech, this Matt Drudge, an uneducated inter-loper, had looked them in the eye and rendered their entire world irrelevant. To those assembled, the speech and Matt's vision of the future was as arrogant as it was obnoxious. And most important, it was wrong. As far as they were concerned, the newspapers and net-work news were at the top of their game, and they weren't about to go anywhere. If anything, they were growing. However, this new fad of internet news was nothing but a flash in the pan, most believed.

"Enjoy your fifteen minutes," a *Washington Post* reporter was heard laughing before walking out the door.

18

FAME

On June 20, 1998, at 8:00 p.m., eastern time, the new television show *Drudge* premiered on the Fox News Channel.

"He's a character," Fox News president Roger Ailes told the *Washington Post*. "He invented himself. He's got a style. At the time I hired him, everyone said I was an idiot and crazy. But he gets it. He's a child of television, computers, and the media."

Matt promised the new show would be lighter than his website and more entertainment driven. In a promotional interview for the show, Matt said, "It will be me, a hat, and the hippest stories on the block . . . I'm going to go wherever the stink is."

For the young man from Takoma Park who had grown up in awe of the entertainment industry, it was yet another peak. "Now I'm getting paid for my own TV show. I'm getting recognized on Sixth Avenue," he continued. "It's been a helluva trip . . . right in front of all the slings and arrows from the crowd, whether from the media or the White House."

Matt's newfound fame marked a shift in his reporting. After Lewinsky, he was no longer content with just getting scoops and reporting them on his website. He had begun exploring ways to shape the broader media narrative. On September 24, 1998, Matt showed up with Arianna Huffington at the embezzlement trial of former Clinton business associate Susan McDougal and crowed over how the *Los Angeles Times* took note of their attendance the next day with a few sentences in the Metro section.

"You can play the media. You can force them to cover things," Andrew Breitbart would later say of the stunt. "This is not just stenography. There's a performance art to it."

In January 1999 Matt again tweaked the media, this time by disclosing that NBC was sitting on reporter Lisa Myers's interview with Juanita Broaddrick, the Arkansas woman who accused Clinton of raping her. Matt had gotten the information straight from Broaddrick, with whom he had developed an online friendship.

As much as Matt enjoyed poking the "mainstream media," the self-proclaimed outsider was suddenly everywhere. On July 9, 1999, it was announced that ABC Radio Networks had signed Matt to anchor a two-hour weekly radio show. ABC News president David Westin strongly objected to the hire but was overruled.

"Matt Drudge is an entertainment brand. He is considered separate from the news side of things," ABC Radio spokeswoman Michelle Bleiberg told CBS News.

Now entrenched in the same corporate mainstream media industrial complex he had been railing against for years, he found himself enjoying the many perks that came with his growing fame. The show would be broadcast from a Washington studio across the street from the Mayflower Hotel, where management upgraded him to a fancy eighth-floor suite. Howard Kurtz wrote in a May 28, 1999, story for the *Washington Post*, "The star treatment is another sign of the burgeoning success that has transformed him from a geek with a gossipy Website to a multimedia phenomenon with a television show, paid lecture dates, a spate of magazine cover stories about him, and a possible movie deal."

And Matt wasn't the only Drudge making headlines. His father, Robert Drudge, was getting acclaim for his own website, Refdesk .com, a free online service that indexed and reviewed web-based resources with "links to dictionaries, newspapers, government sites."

The elder Drudge's upstart site appeared to be the kind of information-based online phenomenon that Matt would promote on the Drudge Report . . . but the link never came.

Robert was "a bit curious as to why for a long time his son did not include a link to Refdesk on his site," read a line in a *New York Times* profile.

"[Matt] said he had no use for Refdesk," Robert told the paper. "He hasn't got time to check things out. He's got to hop, hop, hop and move the story." Matt and his father had decided long ago not to discuss their websites with each other. "We're just focusing on what we do," he told the *Times*, "not on what other people think or say about either of us."

———

New opportunities begat more new opportunities. In one example, a New York brokerage firm offered to put up millions of dollars to finance an online venture with Matt and former Clinton pollster Dick Morris. Matt refused, telling friends he was already financially comfortable. He had moved on from his old Packard Bell to a new black Fujitsu laptop, traded his beat-up Geo Metro for a Corvette, and upgraded his cramped ninth-floor Hollywood apartment for a luxury apartment on Whitley Avenue between Highland and Vine.

Heading for dinner one night, Matt handed Ann Coulter two hundred-dollar bills to pay the taxi driver and told her to keep the change.

"He's constantly giving money away," the conservative columnist said in an interview with the *Washington Post*. "He doesn't know what to do now that he's making money. It's hilarious . . . He's simultaneously larger than life and sort of childlike," said Coulter. "When you ride in the Drudgemobile, he'll play tapes of himself on the radio, and he'll laugh uproariously at his answers. You end up laughing at him laughing at himself."

Not everything changed. Matt kept the same Florsheim shoes and old fedora.

"I'm superstitious and I don't want to rock the boat," Matt would tell friends. "It's a very lucky hat."

All of Matt's newfound good fortune would prove to be short-lived. In November 1999 his career in television came to a crashing end when he refused to show up for a taping after a dispute with network executives over a *National Enquirer* photo of a tiny fetal hand emerging from the womb. Matt wanted to show the picture, which was taken during a spina bifida operation on the fetus, while telling his audience, "Listen, you see this creature with this claw grasping at the doctor's glove? There are operations in this country that kill these creatures—it's called abortion."

Network executives vetoed the idea, saying that portraying that picture with those words would amount to misrepresenting the photo to their Fox News audience. Matt refused to show up for taping, venting to the *Washington Post*: "Over my dead website . . . Seems to me Murdoch has enough money, he doesn't need Drudge money . . . Some of these overgrown fetuses at Fox hit the panic button."

Fox News president Roger Ailes fired back, "He wants to apply internet standards, which are nonexistent, to journalism, and journalism has real standards. It can't work that way."

"I apologize to Fox News for having an open mind," Matt rebutted. "I've been spoiled on the internet, I really have. The lack of ability to express my opinion on an issue that's important to me has left me believing the internet is the future."

The network refused to back down, threatening legal action. Fox attorney Dianne Brandi wrote to him, "You flatly refused to perform the services under your agreement . . . You made disparaging, false and defamatory remarks about Fox News." The letter continued, "It is necessary for you to apologize to Fox News" to avoid the possibility of a breach of contract lawsuit.

However, the abortion controversy wasn't the only sign that the unlikely marriage had run its course. Although usually the network's highest-rated weekend show, *Drudge*'s ratings had dropped 30 percent during the show's first year, from 230,000 to 162,000 households. More significant, the grind of the weekly show had worn Matt down. Privately, he had insinuated that he had precipitated the feud to get out of the final year of his contract. Patrick Manshardt, Matt's attorney, whom he had befriended during the Blumenthal suit, recalled driving Matt to the airport to fly from Los Angeles to New York City for filming.

"The flying coast to coast all the time was a burden. He was ready to end that show. It exhausted him," says Manshardt.

Matt was let out of his contract, but first was forced to apologize to the network.

"In the heat of the moment, in pursuit of a story, I made comments I regret about the innovative Fox News Channel and its executives," he said in a statement.

More bad news came after Matt learned that MSNBC reporter Jeannette Walls had begun research for an upcoming book that promised "a comprehensive, serious exploration of gossip and its social, historical, and political significance," and a look into the major players, including Matt Drudge.

For years, Matt's private life had become the subject of online "rumor campaigns" in internet chat rooms. "They're spreading that I'm a child molester, I'm gay, I've been mentally institutionalized . . .

even rumors of drug use and pornography," he told the *Washington Post*. "All the charges and counter charges on me at some point become just a blur."

A source had informed Matt that Walls's book planned to out him to the public and his conservative audience. Matt fired off a preemptive attack on March 3, 2000, posting an all-caps headline: "MSNBC REPORTER: DRUDGE HAD SEX WITH EGGS."

The article continued, "MSNBC reporter Jeannette Walls is telling associates that she has obtained information linking Matt Drudge with a sexual preference for eggs. 'He likes to have sex with eggs,' Walls told an insider. 'He likes them smeared all over naked male bodies.' Yet another MSNBC exclusive, Walls is also reporting to MSNBC associates that Drudge likes to 'have sex, with his clothes on, in the shower.' Do you have any other Drudge sex stories?"

On March 7, 2000, *Dish: The Inside Story on the World of Gossip* was released with the opening chapter, "Citizen Reporter," divulging modest details of Matt's homosexual lifestyle, albeit without any mention of eggs.

New York *Daily News* gossip columnist George Rush called Matt for comment. "You are in this book and the author suggested that you are gay," Rush told Matt.

"He was quite defensive and denied it," said Rush, who had first met Matt in March 1997 at a party at the Chateau Marmont.

Rush called Walls to let her know that Matt denied the claims made in *Dish*. In response, the author forwarded Rush an email thread she had obtained between Matt and one of his alleged lovers that showed proof of a physical relationship. Rush reached back out to Matt with the evidence, but when confronted with the email, Matt went into overdrive to discredit the reporter.

"Oh, that's fake," said Matt. "Anyone can fake an email by copy and pasting."

He then changed the heading on Rush's email and sent it back to him.

"See," he said. "Easy."

Matt went on to claim Walls's entire account was fabricated. "Jeannette, dear, slow down and come up for some air," he wrote on his site. "You are becoming a laughingstock. Even by MSNBC standards."

Replied Walls, "I'm not passing judgment. But I think his duplicity is relevant to his character as someone who has built his career on exposing others' private lives."

"I go to bars," he later told the *Miami New Times*. "I go to straight bars, I go to gay bars. [Walls] never said there was sex; she said there was dating. She never had enough to go that far."

Asked if it bothered him to be portrayed as gay, Matt answered, "No, because I'm not . . . It's not an issue with me . . . I think I told the *Daily News* something like, "My youth is a blur. That's a good out."

Matt again found himself on the defensive after an avalanche of negative reviews greeted the October 2000 publication of his book, *Drudge Manifesto*. It had been hyped as "the most sensational, the most outspoken, behind-the-scenes story of the year," but critics gleefully slammed the 247-page book, which included forty blank pages, thirty-one pages of fan mail, and nine pages of poetry.

A particularly brutal *Wired* reviewer wrote, "Drudge spends so much time assuring us that he deserves to be taken seriously, it's only natural to come to the opposite conclusion. He deserves to be taken as seriously as the crud on the bottom of your shoe."

Jack Shafer wrote for the *Wall Street Journal*, "Mr. Drudge attempts to chronicle his pioneering internet life and times in *Drudge Manifesto*. But I can't really recommend. His collection. Of sentence fragments. To anybody seeking an intelligible account of. How Drudge. Gave American journalism. A much-needed kick in the tuchas. Besides Mr. Drudge's sentence-fragment tic, he RunsWordsTogetherForDramaticEffect as if under the spell of Lawrence Ferlinghetti, making readers struggle to follow his tale."

Even finding a spot to debut his book became problematic. Matt wanted to personally introduce his book at Politics and Prose, an influential independent DC bookstore he had frequented in his youth, but was shocked to discover that the owners wanted no part of Matt or his book.

"I have literally been told I am not welcome," Matt huffed to the *Washington Post*. "I am going to instruct my publisher not to allow books to be shipped to Politics and Prose."

Bookstore co-owner Carla Cohen told the *Post* that the ban was "not a question of left or right, conservative or liberal. It's a question of sleaze versus careful, thoughtful reporting . . . I think he's a rumormonger and a troublemaker, and I think he's more interested in self-promotion than in journalism."

In spite of the critical backlash after *Drudge Manifesto* was released, it rose to number eight on the *New York Times* bestseller list. Matt reveled in the sales, later telling journalist Geoff Metcalf, "You can just imagine the horror of a lot of those *New York Times* people now having to recognize me in their newspaper as being on their bestseller list."

Matt had another victory in May 2001, when Sidney Blumenthal dropped his lawsuit. Matt told *Salon*, "I never signed off on anything until Blumenthal agreed to pay $2,500 to us, $914 of which was for travel."

Asked what the other $1,586 was used for, Matt replied, "Crow."

———

By the summer of 2001, Matt had achieved a measure of wealth he never could have imagined. He had hosted his own television show, which he could accurately claim as a ratings success; his syndicated radio show was blasting his voice across hundreds of stations; he had published his first book, which despite the negative reviews made the bestseller list; and he had settled the Blumenthal lawsuit, all while continuing to grow one of the most powerful websites in the world.

But Matt's friends began to wonder if something was wrong. They worried that what used to be small glimpses of paranoia were taking a greater hold of Matt's psyche. It didn't help that the Drudge Report tip box had become riddled with hate. He claimed some people wanted him dead. Other messages referenced his sexuality.

After an eavesdropper spotted him in a Los Angeles coffee shop and fed an item on his private conversation to the *New York Post*, Matt began to think there were spies everywhere.

In another example, a camera crew took to the roof of an adjacent building to shoot into Matt's apartment. Matt vented to friends that the Clinton people would never let it go.

19

NEW JOURNALISM

On October 7, 2001, less than one month after the terrorist attacks of 9/11 and eleven months into a new Republican administration, the country was preparing for war when a link appeared in the top left corner of the Drudge Report: "President Bush to Address Nation from Oval Office." Two minutes later the headline mysteriously disappeared. A reporter who saw the flash inquired with sources at the White House and was told it must have been a mistake.

At 1:00 p.m., eastern time, President George W. Bush, still less than one year into his job, made a surprise, nationally televised announcement that the United States military had begun strikes against al-Qaeda terrorist training camps and the Taliban regime in Afghanistan. The speech had been embargoed because of security concerns, and not even the press office was notified until shortly before it was delivered.

The reporter who saw the brief headline on the Drudge Report speculated that someone in the Bush White House had given Drudge a heads-up so Matt would be ready to announce. "Then the White House called and had him pull it back."

The moment was a testament to the perceived power of Matt Drudge. In four short years he had gone from digging through trash for tips to developing an intricate web of sources connected throughout newsrooms from coast to coast and embedded in the deepest corridors of Washington, DC, with congressmen, senators, and even Vice President Dick Cheney soliciting his company.

It was a new brand of journalism, something that no one had ever seen before. And the established media had no idea what to make of any of it. Matt admitted to Howard Kurtz of the *Washington Post* that it all seemed like a "magic show." In one instance, he described using his laptop to tell the world about a Justice Department probe of Ken Starr's office while stuck at an airport in Dallas. He then recalled walking around the terminal "laughing at the absurdity of it all."

Matt openly embraced the idea that his reporting wasn't an exact science. He would run thinly sourced allegations and publish items about people without calling them for comment. After reporting that NBC Washington bureau chief Tim Russert had become upset over his network's failure to report on the Clinton scandals, and in a separate post, writing that Russert was considering a run for governor of New York, Russert shot back, "Just plain dead wrong . . . And he never called me about them, never."

In another instance, at the Radio and Television Correspondents' Dinner in the late '90s, the *Washington Post* reported that Matt got into a spat with Chris Matthews, the host of CNBC's *Hardball*, who accused Matt, once again, of running inaccurate items about him.

"The fact is, you don't get your stories straight when they concern me. Why didn't you call me?" Matthews reportedly asked.

Matt remained unfazed by the criticism, telling Kurtz, "The First Amendment doesn't require you to call people . . . It's probably the Drudge style, to go with what I believe is accurate. Most of the stuff written about me, no one's called . . . I've blown it a few times."

Asked why he doesn't maintain archives of past articles like other sites, he answered, "I don't want the humiliation of having my words coming back to haunt me."

Matt held firm to his conviction that the internet held the future of news. In a May 2002 appearance on CNN's *Crossfire*, host Paul Begala asked Matt if the prediction he had given four years earlier that the mainstream media would be replaced by internet news had been proved wrong. Matt answered, "How many years are we into the internet revolution? Probably five, since Netscape was launched and it became simple with Windows . . . It took hundreds, maybe 150 years for the *New York Times* and others to really catch up to speed to the prominence they have now."

He continued, "It doesn't happen overnight. But I still do see a future where individuals do make a difference, reporting what they know, and what they believe to be true as opposed to corporations and gigantic newsrooms."

When asked by Tucker Carlson how much money he made making the Drudge Report, Matt answered, "Probably more than both of you combined at this table. It's nearly seven figures. And it's a great living because I don't have to share it with anybody. There's no production cost. There's no makeup artist. There's no music, and there's no lighting."

Matt expanded on the power of internet news and the problems inherent in the power of the platform he helped create in a June 2003 interview for *Radar* magazine, telling Camille Paglia, "What scares me is I've got so many smart people reading it: the congressional leaders, the executive branch leaders, the judicial branch leaders, the Hollywood moguls. It's frightening, because it's easy to make mistakes on the internet. You can make up anything about anybody and send it everywhere, all with a hit of the send button."

———

The rules of the news cycle weren't all that was evolving. After spending the two years following his Lewinsky scoop frequenting the interview circuit, friends at the time recall a difference in Matt. His need to be reclusive intensified. He had cut down on his public appearances. He was slower to respond to longtime friends on AOL Instant Messenger. On the increasingly rare occasions Matt did talk to the public, he refused to divulge any details about his life. What started off as a quirk in his personality was now *becoming* his personality.

Picking up on the changes, Paglia asked, "You've been guarded about your personal life, and rarely make the usual media rounds. Why do you stay so mysterious?" Matt deflected from the question. "My private life would make my public persona a lot less interesting . . . Once you take the mask off Batman he seems a bit diminished."

Andrew Breitbart was also starting to ask questions. He was helping to run one of the most influential websites in the world, still helming the nine-to-three shift like clockwork, but months would pass without any communication from his boss.

Breitbart's friend, conservative talk show host John Ziegler, recalls the confusion. "Andrew was both mystified and amazed. Here he was, one of two people running one of the most incredibly powerful enterprises in the world, and they never spoke," says Ziegler. "It was very, very rare for Drudge to communicate."

Sometimes Breitbart would get an out-of-the-blue message from Matt that he would be gone for several days. When he asked where Matt was traveling to, he would be met with radio silence. "At one point Andrew thought he was in Europe. But he was always guessing," adds Ziegler.

The one surefire way to get Matt's attention was to miss a big breaking news story. Ziegler reflects, "If Andrew ever fell asleep at the wheel, Drudge would get really pissed at him and fire off a curt message."

Despite the lack of communication, Breitbart continued working his morning shift with a religious fervor, waking up most days at 6:00 a.m., and then furiously alternating his attention between television news and the wire services, bouncing between different websites, all the while staying on top of emails and the Drudge Report tip box.

Breitbart once explained to Roger Simon, the author and creator of PJ Media, the conservative opinion and commentary blog, that he always needed to be plugged in because the secret to the Drudge Report's success was speed. Even seconds mattered.

"Andrew had figured out how to get the early line for AP," said Simon. "When AP was breaking, Andrew and Matt were jumping on AP faster than other people. That was part of their original plan. Speed was very important to them."

However, the tension from always having to be plugged in was taking its toll on Breitbart, recalls Ziegler: "It was incredibly stressful. He felt like a goalkeeper. Just making sure nothing got past him. Andrew had to be wired in all the time. If he was going into his sports bar, he would be watching the Dodgers game while monitoring news."

Stress over finances was also beginning to take its toll on Breitbart. He had long recognized the mistake he had made in turning down Matt's offer to be a partner in the Drudge Report. It cost him millions of dollars, but the monthly personal checks from Matt were barely enough to cover Andrew's expenses.

A friend of Breitbart's remembers, "Andrew couldn't figure it out. There was no reason for it. Sometimes he'd be killing it with traffic and the site would be making millions and millions of dollars and a check for just a few thousand dollars would show up in the mail."

His friends encouraged him to confront Matt to demand an increase in pay and a contract, but Breitbart was reluctant. Matt's increasingly reclusive behavior had made him nearly unapproachable. According to Ziegler, "In Andrew's mind, it was as if Drudge had become this Howard Hughes kind of character."

Matt's isolation hadn't just alienated Breitbart. In one instance, after Matt let it slip to an acquaintance where he was traveling, Matt suddenly became unhinged, screaming that the person would betray him by revealing his travel destination to the world. It was the last time the two would ever speak.

"Everything okay?" another longtime friend messaged him in 2002. Matt never responded.

20

FLORIDA

By 2002 Matt Drudge had made the decision to move to Florida. He had tired of the high state income tax and the grueling traffic. One afternoon, after getting stuck at the corner of Highland Avenue and Sunset Boulevard, he got so frustrated by the congestion that he considered leaving his car in the middle of the street. He described the scene as "a nightmare, like a scene from Joel Schumacher's *Falling Down*"—a movie about a man who loses it after his car breaks down in traffic.

It was during his search for Sunshine State real estate that Matt first came across a Florida-based real estate blog that piqued his interest. He sent an email to the man who ran the blog, Kevin Tomlinson. The two agreed to meet up and clicked immediately over a shared passion for the vibrant Miami club scene.

"We bonded over music," recalls Tomlinson. "I used to be a DJ, and he was very fond of club music."

Through Tomlinson, Matt purchased a two-bedroom, two-bathroom condo at the Four Seasons in Miami Beach. During the negotiations, the real estate agent was struck by Matt's thoughtfulness. "Matt was a very strategic negotiator, but he did not want to offend anyone. He always cared about that. It was unusual for a client to be so considerate of everyone else involved in a transaction."

The two began to spend time together socially, and Tomlinson was quickly made aware of Matt's fame. "Everyone was saying, 'Oh, this is the guy who broke the Monica scandal.' I didn't really care about any of that. I wasn't very political."

However, Tomlinson would discover the power of the Drudge Report after getting the scoop that Miami Heat star Shaquille O'Neal had signed a contract to pay about $22 million for the seventeen-thousand-square-foot mansion built by the son of billionaire H. Wayne Huizenga on the Intracoastal Waterway in Fort Lauderdale. Tomlinson posted the news on his website, and Matt linked to the story. In an instant, the influx of traffic took down Tomlinson's site. "One link and it crashed every server I had," says Tomlinson.

After explaining to Matt what the traffic had done to his website, Matt broke out in laughter, telling Tomlinson, "If you are going to play in the big leagues, you've got to step up."

———

Matt was delighting in the power and scope of his creation. Despite his self-imposed exile from the public eye, his website continued to achieve new highs, and Matt couldn't resist the temptation to use his unprecedented page views as a weapon to poke at the media establishment that had all too frequently lambasted him.

On November 13, 2002, Matt crowed,

OVER 1 BILLION SERVED IN PAST YEAR: The WALL STREET JOURNAL declared "Matt Drudge a born loser," the NEW YORK TIMES last week in a Page One story claimed people have been "reduced to logging onto the Web site of the gossip columnist Matt Drudge," but in every state and nearly every civilized nation in the developed world, readers know where to go for action and reaction of news—at least one day ahead. Sometime this afternoon, the DRUDGEREPORT will pass one billion views of the site's main page: in the past year! Free from any corporate concerns, there are simply too many to thank since the site's inception in 1994. This new attempt at the old American experiment of full freedom in reporting is ever exciting. Those in power have everything to lose by individuals who march to their own rules . . .

The number of page views was stunning, even when considering the natural inflation resulting from the home page's automatic refreshing, which happened every 2 minutes and 55 seconds. Matt boasted that it was the Drudge name that brought eyeballs to his page, telling Tomlinson, "The interesting thing about my website is that I don't need to create content. I just link to content. And they come to me because I'm Matt Drudge."

Matt presented himself as a contradiction. He shunned attention while enjoying the fame. He also enjoyed letting people know that he wouldn't bend, no matter who was doing the asking. In one example, actor George Clooney was filming *K Street*, his upcoming HBO television series about lobbyists and politicians in Washington, DC, when producers reached out to Matt to ask permission to show the Drudge Report on a computer screen in the background of a scene. Matt never responded, so Clooney obtained Matt's cell phone number and personally called. Matt refused. Clooney politely persisted.

"Has anyone ever told you no, George Clooney? No, George Clooney! No!" Matt claimed to have responded.

―――――――

By the mid-2000s, South Florida had become a small enclave for conservative leaders. In 2003 Matt's circle of friends had continued to dwindle, but one relationship he kept was with conservative commentator Ann Coulter, who became his neighbor, moving into a penthouse in the same building.

Matt and Coulter would sometimes visit Rush Limbaugh's gated oceanfront compound in Palm Beach, staying in one of his five guesthouses. Limbaugh's brother, David, would occasionally help Matt with legal work.

Chris Ruddy, who had become inspired by Matt during their dinner together in the mid-1990s, had also planted his growing conservative media empire in Florida. After hearing Matt describe the scope of the Drudge Report's readership during their dinner together in 1994, Ruddy went to his boss, *Pittsburgh Tribune-Review* publisher Richard Mellon Scaife, and proposed starting an internet newspaper.

"I saw the power and influence that he [Matt] had developed on the internet. He was a genius. I thought I could turn it into a business model," says Ruddy. Scaife declined. Ruddy left the *Tribune-Review* and took stories that were not published online, printed them out, and began setting up an email list for distribution. Before long, he had ten thousand subscribers paying thirty dollars a year. That success led him to begin the conservative website Newsmax in 1998. Five years later, Newsmax was flourishing. Ruddy set up headquarters in West Palm Beach with a massive $8.55 million, 61,900-square-foot office building.

Ruddy was joined in South Florida by conservative headliners such as former secretary of education Bill Bennett, former Reagan adviser Larry Kudlow, and Speaker of the House Newt Gingrich. Gay Gaines, a longtime GOP political operative, would host fundraisers where Limbaugh, Bennett, Kudlow, Gingrich, and other GOP bold names would stay up until two in the morning partying. Matt was always invited, but never came.

"We would love to get Matt," Gaines told the *New York Times*. "But he doesn't like appearing at fundraisers."

Matt Drudge had become a nighttime fixture in the vibrant South Beach club scene, where once again, his personal life became a popular topic of conversation.

"Everybody talked about Matt's sexuality," recalls Tomlinson. "I mean, here was one of the heads of the conservative movement and he was openly gay. It was hard for people to get their heads around it."

Matt had been dating for several years, but finally entered into a long-term relationship with a real estate agent and mutual friend of Tomlinson's. "Matt seemed happy. It was clear they really clicked and had a good relationship. I was happy for him."

But soon Matt's personal life once again made the headlines. In August 2002, actor Alec Baldwin told the *Howard Stern Show* that Matt had hit on him in a "creepy" way after a chance meeting in a hallway at ABC Studios.

"He came right up to me and he looked like he had a fork and knife in each of his hands. He said, 'Do you have any Tabasco sauce? I want to drizzle it all over you,'" said Baldwin.

Matt released a statement saying, "This is a guy whose career is in turnaround, and his mind is not holding up well. I've never met Alec Baldwin. If he has fantasies about being cruised by guys maybe he can star in *Cruising Part 2: The Troll Years*."

He added that he had considered suing the actor for slander but ultimately decided against it. "My lawyer tells me what [he] said about me is actionable, but does Alec have any cash left to collect damages?"

In an interview with blogger Brandon Moss, Baldwin appeared taken aback by Matt's response. "I just remember thinking, 'Why is he so uptight about being gay? Who's worried about that anymore?' And I wasn't calling him gay. I just said he hit on me, which I found unusual. Because he's somebody who could vilify me politically, but he sure didn't seem like he wanted to vilify me when we were in the hallway. And maybe he's not gay. Maybe he just had some sort of moment there in the hallway."

Following the public back-and-forth, friends say Matt began to further insulate himself from the public. After a lunch with *Washington Post* columnist Lloyd Grove, Matt had invited him to see the new house he had purchased in South Florida. Grove agreed and they piled into Matt's pickup truck to drive to the island.

Grove had formed a friendly working relationship with Matt after meeting him in the '90s at a *Vanity Fair* Oscar party. Matt would frequently stop by and visit Grove when he was working as a gossip columnist at the New York *Daily News*. Later, when Grove ran the column Reliable Sources, Matt would call with questions about journalistic ethics.

Grove naturally assumed Matt meant he wanted to show him the inside of the home, but when they stopped in front of the residence, Matt didn't get out of the car.

"Aren't you going to show me the inside of the house?" asked Grove.

"No," Matt answered curtly.

Matt immediately drove Grove back to the restaurant where his car was waiting.

"It was all very strange," Grove recalls.

By early 2007 Matt had stopped wearing his fedora, telling Grove that he didn't like the attention. "He was triaging his relationships and streamlining his life to a point where he would only engage with people he found essential to his life."

———

A revealing *New York* magazine piece written by Philip Weiss, published on August 24, 2007, further stoked Matt's paranoia. In the article, Weiss used quotes from Matt's radio show, giving the story the feel of an interview. Twenty-four hours after the story hit the web, Matt removed the link to his radio show entirely from the Drudge Report. Ten days later, it was announced that a new anchor had been hired for the 325 stations that broadcast his Sunday night show and that Matt would soon be quitting.

A few days after the story was published Matt met up for drinks with a work-related acquaintance and confided that he was ready to go completely off the grid. "I'm thinking of just going dark. So there is no longer a face to the Drudge Report," he said. "This page would do better if I disappear. If I don't exist. If there is no target."

On September 30, 2007, after nine years and nearly five hundred shows, Matt Drudge signed off from his radio show for the final time, but not before delivering one final message to his radio audience, venting about the media's "obsession" with him.

> I've been here working all the time. And I mean all the time. All this stuff you're hearing from other people: "Oh, Drudge has, you know, he has hired a team of people doing it now. He's not even updating anymore." That's ridiculous. Andrew does it for a few hours a day. Sometimes more than that. I'm always here. Always here working. Always studying the news and the headlines and the information and the emails here which are up to about 15,000 a day on some hot days. Very involved in the flow of the internet and the media cycles in general so I haven't stepped down. All of that has been erroneous, jealous reporting. When your competition reports on you—and I consider my competition to be anybody from the news business—you've got to take that for what it is.

Matt had been dishing out scoops and often exposing personal details of people's lives from nearly the first time he fired off a Drudge Report email. He had survived the many slings and arrows tossed his way, especially after breaking the Lewinsky story. But for Matt, this article was different. The people who had attacked him in the past had their sights set on the persona he had created and hid behind as the eccentric, fedora-wearing creator of the Drudge Report. He believed this article crossed a line. Despite the article being largely flattering, Matt felt this was personal. The man who for years had felt the world opening to him now felt the walls closing in.

21

HILLARY

The Clinton war machine was worried. Hillary Clinton's path to the nomination was facing a significant hurdle from North Carolina senator John Edwards. During the January 3, 2008, Iowa caucuses, the first contest of the nomination process, Edwards had placed second with 30 percent of the vote to Illinois senator Barack Obama, who finished with 38 percent. Clinton had come in third place with 29 percent of the vote.

They needed to take Edwards out, and the thinking inside the Clinton war room was that it would just be a matter of time. The campaign had learned that Edwards had been carrying on an affair with Rielle Hunter, whom he had hired to film a webisode called "Plane Truths," all while his wife, Elizabeth, was fighting cancer. More damning still, Hunter was pregnant with Edwards's child. However, the Clinton team was in a bind. They needed the story to drop, but because of Bill Clinton's past they realized they couldn't be the first to do it. They were waiting on Matt Drudge.

"We knew Matt had the story," a senior Clinton campaign staffer said. "We just weren't sure when he was going to drop it. We just kept refreshing the Drudge Report and waiting."

———

The Drudge Report and its publisher first began wielding political influence nearly a decade earlier, in 1999, when right-leaning politicians saw the website as a way to get their message through to the public without having to go through the filter of a mainstream media they believed to be adversarial.

Tim Griffin was a twenty-nine-year-old staffer on the House Committee on Government Reform when the GOP first employed the Drudge Report while working on an investigation into Chinese influence during the Clinton campaign.

"I had never heard of Matt Drudge until he broke the Monica Lewinsky story in 1998, but I immediately wanted to meet him and understand how his revolutionary use of the internet could help us communicate our message," remembers Griffin.

At the time, the committee was investigating the forty-three-year-old Taiwanese-born businessman Johnny Chung, but it had run into a wall. Chung agreed to plead guilty to charges in March 1998, which included funneling $20,000 in illegal contributions to the Clinton-Gore reelection campaign, but the Republican-controlled committee needed Citibank to release records to show where the money was flowing. The bank was refusing to hand over the information.

The committee released a letter it had written to Citibank following up on a subpoena for bank records to the public. Matt understood its import and picked it up.

"Drudge published the letter and wrote a story about it, which put pressure on Citibank to release the records we had subpoenaed as part of our investigation of Chinese money flowing through

American donors into the Democratic National Committee," according to Griffin.

After appearing on the Drudge Report, the story began to cycle through the media, ramping up pressure on the bank. Soon after, the records were handed over. "It would have taken a lot longer to get those records if it wasn't for Matt Drudge."

When Tim Griffin left the committee to become head of research for the Republican National Committee in August 1999, he brought along his relationship with Matt.

In 2000 Matt helped defeat Al Gore by highlighting Gore's fundraising appearance at a Buddhist temple. In 2004 he helped defeat John Kerry by shining a spotlight on his Vietnam service with the "Swift boat" controversy. During both campaign cycles, Griffin was extremely active using the Drudge Report.

Griffin's system was simple. When they needed a story to get out into the mainstream, they would first go to a reporter from the *Washington Post*, under the condition that a teaser would first go to the Drudge Report. It was a win-win. Griffin would get his story amplified, the reporter would get more page views, and Matt would have his exclusive.

"The Drudge Report vastly increased the reach of any story to help maximize coverage," says Griffin.

The link alone was only part of the benefit. Once posted, an article on the Drudge Report would create more media as other news organizations would race to replicate what Matt had posted in hopes of piggybacking off his web traffic.

Griffin also got to know Matt personally, and the two would occasionally meet for a drink. He described Matt as "extraordinarily intelligent and driven."

"He was a disruptor who challenged conventions . . . a pioneer and a visionary in the world of communications," said Griffin.

In early 2005 Griffin facilitated a passing of the baton. He was transitioning to the White House, and Matt Rhoades, who had never met Matt, was taking over. Griffin, Rhoades, and former Republican National Committee communications director Jim Dyke met Matt at the exclusive Miami steakhouse the Forge. The meeting was a success.

And the cycle continued.

———

By 2007 Hillary Clinton's war room had made the decision that the reach of Matt Drudge's influence outweighed any bad blood that had accumulated over the years from the Clinton-Lewinsky saga. No longer could they afford to look at Matt Drudge as the enemy. He was simply too powerful. Instead, a concerted effort was made to harness the power of the Drudge Report. They went to work trying to cultivate a relationship of their own with the elusive web publisher.

The goal was to create a mutually beneficial arrangement in the same way the GOP had done. The Clinton camp could push favorable items into the news cycle, while Matt would receive an increase in traffic. A former senior Clinton campaign official recalls,

> In the war room when we had something to drop on an opponent that was kind of sleazy and couldn't take it to a legitimate news network, we would call in [a staffer] and he would take it to Drudge. What was key for us was having a relationship. We would pick up the phone and say we have something for you.
>
> Drudge was just an outlet for us to really get news that mainstream media would not normally take. In order to get that done we had people dedicated to schmoozing the guy, calling him, making sure we were massaging his ego. Whatever it took.

Campaign officials said Phil Singer and Howard Wolfson both communicated with Matt, but over the course of the campaign there was only one person able to develop a personal relationship: Tracy Sefl, who advised Team Clinton on national media strategy and tactics.

Sefl first met Matt at a White House Correspondents' Association dinner weekend party in 2004, when she had been a war room staffer for the DNC, doing rapid response and opposition research on both George W. Bush and Dick Cheney. Afterward, Sefl and Drudge began to exchange messages over AOL Messenger. "I was working seven days a week. He was always online," says Sefl.

Sefl believes Matt took a liking to her because she wasn't a seasoned politico. "I didn't come out of the world of campaigns. I had come right out of graduate school. I think he could sense that maybe I was somehow different. I didn't have any 'Drudge baggage' from other campaigns." Meanwhile, Sefl found Matt droll, observant, and funny.

Through Sefl, the Clinton campaign was able to accomplish their goal of leveraging the Drudge Report's influence over the news cycle to their advantage. "We had a very familiar and very regular relationship for a long time. At times, we were in communication nearly every day. When he was about to post a story that wasn't going in Hillary's favor, I always got a heads-up, and sometimes I was able to convince him to change something. Sometimes I wasn't," says Sefl.

If Sefl heard a stray quote she thought might be of interest to Matt, she messaged him. Matt would put it up as a teaser without a link. In one instance she overheard, "Obama had just said something about not using nukes. I let Matt know what I heard. Matt posted: "Obama: No nukes." However, what Matt loved scooping the rest of the media on was fundraising numbers. Sefl was happy to oblige, so long as it was to the benefit of her candidate.

In one instance, after Obama had raised more first-quarter money for the primary race than Clinton, the campaign preemptively leaked an exclusive claiming she had raised $36 million. As Obama prepared to give a major speech on Iraq, a flashing red-siren alert went up on the Drudge Report website above the banner headlines "Queen of the Quarter: Hillary Crushes Obama in Surprise Fund-Raising Surge" and "$27 Million, Sources Tell Drudge Report."

The strategic leak shifted focus from Obama's speech back to Clinton. Inside the campaign, the headline was seen as a huge win. Matt bragged to Sefl that even his old nemesis, former President Bill Clinton, approved of Matt's coverage, saying he got wind of the former president saying, "It's about time Drudge did something fair."

In another example, the campaign fed Matt a link to a story in which Michelle Obama hit Hillary Clinton over Bill's infidelity. The story presented Obama in an unflattering light, with a link to an exclusive videotape of her comment.

"Matt and I had an odd but mutual respect for each other. He was very big on sending me stories before they were published. He obviously was getting things from people other than byline reporters. He had people at editorial desks and the copy desks feeding him," said Sefl.

Sefl also became keenly aware of the importance Matt put on privacy. When, in October 2007, Sefl was contacted by *New York Times* reporter Jim Rutenberg, letting her know he was going to write a story about their unlikely alliance, Sefl immediately called Matt.

"I had learned the story was coming, and I told Matt I wasn't going to comment. He asked me what I thought he should do. I think he was sincerely asking. I told him I didn't think he should comment, either. He didn't," said Sefl.

In spite of their silence, the relationship between Matt and Sefl was outed in the most public way imaginable on October 22, 2007, in a front page *New York Times* headline: "Clinton Finds Way to Play Along with Drudge."

"The Democrats have come to believe," the article read, "what Republicans have always thought: No single person is more relevant to shaping the media environment in a political campaign."

The article continued, "Few are willing to attach their names to any specific statements about Mr. Drudge or descriptions of their strategies in dealing with him, fearing that they might alienate him . . . A strategist close to the Clinton campaign said, her aides had decided to use the site more aggressively and capitalize on the line to him established by Ms. Sefl."

The second the story broke on the *Times* website it went viral, spawning coverage of the unlikely alliance all around the world.

"That *New York Times* story had international impact," said Sefl. "Reporters were mesmerized. That part of it was kind of fun. I also thought some of it was envy. At the time, every reporter was dying to get a link on Drudge."

Clinton's competitors also took note of the unlikely alliance. "The Clinton campaign clearly had an ability to move negative stuff about Edwards and Obama in a way that we did not have," Joe Trippi, chief strategist to John Edwards, told the UK *Telegraph*. "They tried to take some of the tactics that had worked against them and use them for their own gain just as people were growing sick of the kind of politics that's about what's the next bucket of blood that's going to be dumped on Drudge."

But as every campaign learned, a relationship with Matt doesn't always work out as intended. On February 25, 2008, a picture showing Obama in a turban during a 2006 visit to Kenya first appeared on the Drudge Report. Matt posted the image along with a published note on his website that he received the email from a Hillary Clinton staffer, who asked, "Wouldn't we be seeing this on the cover of every magazine if it were HRC?" But Matt had his information wrong. The email had come from a volunteer in Iowa. Not a staffer.

"An unpaid field organizer who sent the link to her friend and told her to spread it around. From there, someone got it to Drudge," said a former senior Clinton official.

The campaign let go of the volunteer, but the damage had already been done. Within hours, the insinuation that Clinton was attempting to dredge up racial animus against the first major African American candidate had funneled its way through the conservative echo chamber and into the mainstream media, dominating the news cycle for days.

The national media immediately descended on Sefl, knowing of her connection to Matt. "I had nothing to do with this, but not surprisingly, the media were coming to me asking if I had anything to do with that photo. I was hugely offended. It was such a juvenile move. In the moment, it caused a lot of hand-wringing. It really was upsetting."

The Drudge Report post infuriated the Clinton war room. Sefl recalls, "Clinton staffers would say to me, 'At the end of the day he is still a Republican. He will still fuck us when he can fuck us.'"

Sefl didn't like the headline but had understood all along that Matt's loyalty wasn't to any candidate but to his page. She saw it as Matt's form of comedy. "Matt thinks this is hilarious. For him, the Drudge Report was performance art, replete with comedy and tragedy and cliffhangers and suspense," says Sefl. "It's the Matt show."

Only three days after publishing the Obama picture, the "Matt show" sparked outrage once again . . . this time after reporting the news that Prince Harry of the British royal family was serving in Afghanistan.

"They're calling him 'Harry the Hero!'" proclaimed the Drudge Report.

Condemnation poured in from all corners of the globe. Angry internet users changed the Drudge Report's Wikipedia page to describe it as an "irresponsible and ill-advised 'news' website that has seen fit to put the lives of many soldiers at risk by publishing reports of Prince Harry's deployment in Afghanistan." The mayor of Windsor and Maidenhead formally called for Matt to apologize. Matt never responded to the mayor or the avalanche of negative media that followed. Instead, he watched from a distance, often calling Sefl and asking for her impression of things that were written about him.

"Usually, we would laugh," Sefl remembers. "He would almost always say no one had any idea what they were talking about."

As Matt's trust grew, they began to spend time together. Matt invited Tracy to his condo, picking her up at her hotel in his black

Mustang so she wouldn't burn in the Miami sun. She recalled that the drive from her hotel to Matt's condo was "slightly terrifying."

"The Mustang was all tricked out on the inside with the middle console taken up by a laptop, if I remember correctly, plugged in so he could be online while driving. He was always online. He would type while driving."

After arriving at the building, Matt first stopped at his mailbox in the lobby and pulled out a thick pile of mail. He told Sefl it was all lawsuits. He couldn't care less. It was such a constant for him. "That was his life: come home, open the mail, chuck the lawsuits over on the counter," said Sefl.

The apartment was sparse, sleek, and modern, with a refrigerator filled with cases of Diet Pepsi.

"I was very flattered that he invited me into his home. That spoke volumes. He once told me I was only the third woman, the first being his mother, the second being Ann Coulter, who had ever been inside," says Sefl. "That's not a list I ever thought I'd be on."

Another time they went out to eat at a "swanky place" in Miami. Nobody bothered them. When they met, they talked about his business, hotel recommendations, and their shared love of cats. "The kittens were his children. They were very important to him."

Matt shared with Sefl his passion for traveling, once expressing his love for Tel Aviv, and frequently asked for her opinion on how the media covered him. In one instance, Matt scoffed while discussing the book *The Way to Win* by Mark Halperin and the *Washington Post*'s John Harris in which an entire chapter was devoted to Matt, anointing him "the Walter Cronkite of his era." He told Sefl that if he ever decided to tell his own story, it would look nothing like Halperin's book.

He also talked about his father's health problems and his discussions with politicians, recounting the time when House Speaker Nancy Pelosi thought he still lived in Los Angeles. Annoyed, Matt told Pelosi to "update her files, I have been in Miami for seven years."

Sefl was also aware of Matt's reputation as a recluse. His communication could be erratic. At times he would inexplicably "go dark." According to Sefl, "He was my buddy. A very important buddy who was sometimes terrifying. But my buddy."

As spring turned to fall, the Clinton campaign was still refreshing their browsers in hopes of seeing news of John Edwards's indiscretions on the Drudge Report.

It never did.

22

HUFFPO

On the evening of September 7, 2001, Andrew Breitbart sent an AOL instant message to his friend, journalist Marc Ebner.

"Turn on your television to ABC," Breitbart wrote under his handle "bodiaz."

Ebner turned his screen on to see Anne Heche being interviewed by Barbara Walters on *20/20* when the actress suddenly broke out speaking in an alien language: "Oh, Quiness, ah ka fota tuna dunna."

Ebner was stunned.

> MarkEbner59: You've got to be kidding me! This is about the most insane thing I have seen on TV—ever . . . I can't believe that ABC is running this for an hour under the guise of news!

Bodiaz: I think you should pitch a magazine piece. Call it "Hollywood, Interrupted"—a play off the award-winning Jolie/Ryder real life nutcase review. Celebrities are now reveling in their madness, and for the first time in history getting paid big dollars to be anti-role models. It's "insanity chic."

Ebner loved the idea. But instead of a magazine piece titled "Hollywood, Interrupted," the two decided to write a book. It would become a *New York Times* bestseller.

"You can tell who wrote which chapter. If it had the stamp of moral outrage on it, that would be Andrew," says Ebner.

The two toured the country and Canada together. One night, Breitbart pulled Ebner over to his computer. "Let me show you something," he said.

Breitbart opened up the Drudge Report and put a link up to their book on the site.

"Watch," he said.

Moments later the link disappeared. Matt had taken it down.

Breitbart shrugged. "Oh well."

Promoting *Hollywood, Interrupted* on the Drudge Report had been part of the agreement Breitbart and Ebner had made with the publishing house.

"It might have only been for a few minutes but now he could cross that off the list," says Ebner.

———

On the road, Ebner and Breitbart discussed politics, life, and on occasion, working for Matt Drudge.

Breitbart's morning shift for the Drudge Report was all consuming. Even while on the road for the book tour, Breitbart had to stay plugged in to the website. Matt was even more obsessive than he was, according to Breitbart, but shared that he did have at least one vice.

"Matt was a big gambler," says Ebner. "He liked to go down to the seediest casinos, the ones that were off-strip. He would go and play the high-end slots. The hundred-dollar slots. He would sit there for hours pulling the lever."

Through Breitbart, Ebner eventually forged his own relationship with Matt. He appeared as a guest on Matt's radio show, and soon after, found himself on the receiving end of Matt's erratic AOL messages. In one instance, Ebner logged on to his computer to see a message from mDrudge that simply read "Pick up your phone."

A moment later his phone rang. He picked it up. Then another message appeared: "Put it on speaker." Ebner did as instructed.

"The next thing I know, I'm listening to the gnarliest hard-core gangster rap you could ever imagine. I had never in all my life heard anything like it. What he was playing for me was an underground hip-hop guerrilla station that was broadcast out of a truck cruising through Miami. It was absolutely unreal," says Ebner. "The guy is a hard-core Miami music fan. Now who would think this guy Matt Drudge would be into that?"

Breitbart thrived during his time with Ebner on the book tour. It was an opportunity for him to get out from behind the Drudge Report, and once surrounded by like-minded, right-leaning thinkers, Breitbart was in his element. Ebner could sense that Breitbart was enjoying his moment in the limelight more than the anonymity of working under Matt, and once asked him what he wanted to do with his life.

"I want to be a pundit," Breitbart answered.

Much of the groundwork for Breitbart's eventual foray into media had already been laid. As a sometime gatekeeper of the Drudge Report, he had forged close contacts with some of the country's leading politicians, media members, and key conservative figures, and now he had a *New York Times* bestseller under his belt.

Hollywood, Interrupted had further launched Breitbart's profile into the public sector among the conservative base. But his growing name recognition and his bestselling book weren't enough to pull him out of the financial debt he had accumulated from a series of costly home renovations and other expenses. The personal checks sent monthly from Matt's personal checking account no longer sufficed.

After the 2004 election Breitbart was approached by Arianna Huffington to be one of four partners to help launch a new website, the Huffington Post.

Huffington, who left the Republican Party in 1996 to become a progressive Democrat, said her vision was to write a group blog that would range in topics from politics and entertainment to sports and religion. Instead of aggregating news and opinion like the Drudge Report, the HuffPo would host it. Newswires would appear right on the site. Bloggers from the left and right could voice their opinions in a giant group forum. Breitbart had forged a personal relationship with Huffington when he interned for her. Most important for his work in developing the site, he was offered a 2 to 3 percent ownership of the new venture.

In a solicitation letter to her contacts, Huffington said the site "Won't be left wing or right wing; indeed, it will punch holes in that very stale way of looking at the world."

———

A friend of Breitbart's recalls the conflicted feelings Breitbart had over the thought of parting ways with the Drudge Report: "Breitbart had high anxiety about going to the Huffington Post, but he needed the money."

Breitbart rationalized that if he handled the blog side and stayed away from news aggregation then he wouldn't be directly competing with the Drudge Report, and would, in turn, manage to avoid Matt's wrath. Breitbart held his breath and took the plunge, telling friends, "I think it will be okay with Matt."

On April 25, 2005, the *New York Times* ran a piece that stated, in part, that the Huffington Post was a direct challenge to the Drudge Report.

"In fact," the story stated, "she has hired away Mr. Drudge's right-hand Web whiz, Andrew Breitbart, who used to be her researcher."

The reporter reached out to Matt, who emailed back that he was "excited" for Huffington. "The internet is still in its infancy," he said. "It's wide open." But privately, Matt was seething.

On April 26, 2005, Breitbart released a statement to Roger Simon's blog: "I am amicably leaving the Drudge Report after a long and close working relationship with Matt Drudge, a man who will rightfully take his place in the history books as an internet news pioneer. I am also excited to be a partner in an inspired new endeavor, the Huffington Post. The last time I worked with Arianna, she got a guy who didn't deserve to be buried in Arlington National Cemetery disinterred. That was cool. I admit: I like to go where the action is."

In the note, Breitbart described himself as "a raucous, opinionated, red meat eating libertarian-leaning conservative who refuses to be relegated to a conservative ghetto," but added,

> The last election cycle gave me an ulcer. As a Dennis Miller/ *South Park* kind of Republican, I am offended by both 'Bush Is Hitler' rhetoric and fetus-in-a-jar political speech. What the world needs more of is amicable—even jocular— disagreement. Bringing my former boss and longtime friend Arianna's intriguing friends to the blogosphere, the ultimate level playing field, makes perfect sense to me, and I am thrilled to be committed to such a groundbreaking project.

That spring, Breitbart traveled from his Los Angeles home to the SoHo offices in New York City, where he worked closely with Ken Lerer and Jonah Peretti, a graduate of MIT's media lab, to launch the site.

In an interview with BuzzFeed News, Peretti remembered that Breitbart "was terrified of the idea that the Huffington Post was a competitor to Drudge."

"He was at war with himself," Peretti said. "He wanted to be sure Drudge respected what he did and that he could also make this new venture. He thought that the Huffington Post could be bipartisan and that Drudge would love the idea of these big boldface names blogging because he understands the value of that."

Breitbart had tried to convince himself that the launch of the Huffington Post could actually work to Matt's benefit. He had also hoped to persuade Matt to monetize some of his outgoing links by starting a kind of "Drudgewire."

For decades, news agency organizations like Reuters and the Associated Press, which gathered news reports and sold them to newspapers, magazines, and radio and television broadcasters for a subscription fee, had played a dominant role in the media landscape. Breitbart, who perceived the wire services as extensions of the Democratic Party, believed that the market existed for him to create his own wire service that would feature more right-leaning articles. He also realized that it would be a tough sell to Matt.

———————

Shortly after the Huffington Post launched on May 9, 2005, the website not only took a leftward tilt but also heavily relied on news aggregation, making it a clear and direct competitor to Drudge. The relationship soured. By that June, Breitbart was out. He made another disastrous business decision when he decided to take a small buyout instead of the percentage he was originally promised, which would have been worth millions if Breitbart had waited.

Breitbart went back to work for Matt, knowing that he wasn't going to pay him more, but offering "four or five ideas on how to make money." Idea number one was to buy a subscription to the newswire services. To Breitbart, it made perfect sense. On any given week the Drudge Report would link to hundreds of wire stories, sending traffic, along with the advertising revenue that accompanied it, to third parties. If they bought into the wires, Breitbart reasoned, that money could be kept in-house.

"The idea was to have ten wire services and have them all under Breitbart.com," says a friend of Breitbart's. "If you were someone who wanted to be inside the news, this would be the ultimate news junkie page."

Matt shot the idea down, telling Breitbart, "Then the Drudge Report would become a business, and the Drudge Report will never be a business."

But Breitbart came back with a counteroffer: What if he fronted the money himself to buy the wires under his name? Would Matt then agree to allow him to link to the wires he owned?

Matt signed off on the deal. Breitbart moved forward with purchasing a subscription to the wire services, telling friends he took out loans totaling $150,000 for the subscription. In the summer of 2005, he launched Breitbart.com, "providing up-to-the-minute wire service stories."

Publicly, Breitbart said that he "wanted to create the single best place where I could go as an avid news reader to get headlines the second they hit the internet so I don't have to go to forty sites." When asked if there had been an agreement with the Drudge Report, Breitbart told reporters, "I'm grateful for the traffic that is sent my way."

The new arrangement would dramatically change the composition of the Drudge Report. On August 17, 2005, Breitbart.com went live. On August 29, 2005, Breitbart peppered the Drudge Report with links from Breitbart.com forty-eight times, according to an analysis by Kalev Leetaru, a researcher at the University of Illinois Cline Center for Democracy. By flooding the Drudge Report with links to Breitbart's wire page, Breitbart.com went from obscurity to boasting 2.64 million unique visitors in its first month of operation, according to Nielsen/NetRatings.

Publicly, Matt said he was happy to assist his friend, telling CNET News, "For the wire stories, I've always looked for places with low graphics, without a lot of spinning Java tops on them . . . When I send my readers someplace, I want it to be convenient for them to get there." He added, "I want to help him out. He has always wanted to do this. This is his idea and hopefully he can make a living from it."

———

Breitbart had other revenue ideas. He entered into a pay-per-click financial arrangement with Reuters that further altered the page. From January 1, 2005, to October 14, 2005, the Drudge Report linked just twenty-nine times to Reuters. In the period following the deal, from October 15, 2005, to December 31, 2005, the Drudge Report linked to Reuters.com 229 times.

Each Reuters link was embedded with an HTML tag that allowed the news agency to track how much revenue Breitbart had been generating by the traffic sent their way. While Matt never explicitly said that Breitbart wasn't allowed to use the coded links, he voiced his displeasure in other ways.

"Drudge didn't like it," says Ziegler. "He would go on and replace the coded links with links that had no code. It made Andrew furious. Matt was so passive-aggressive. Breitbart would be like, 'That bastard did it again! That bastard took down my links!'"

It wasn't the only pay-for-play arrangement. On January 26, 2006, Breitbart and his wife were sued by the Minnesota-based internet advertising firm Gen Ads for $75,000 for allegedly being in violation of their own agreement to take advantage of Drudge Report traffic. The court papers outlined a process of how Breitbart was able to manipulate the Drudge Report website to line his own pockets. According to court documents, after the August 2005 launch, Breitbart.com almost immediately became one of the most trafficked sites on the internet, with 2.64 million visits in its first month of operation. Nearly all the traffic originated from his own referrals while helming the Drudge Report.

The advertising agency was happy with the traffic until it learned that Breitbart had broken the agreement by promoting a third party: "In November 2005, Gen Ads learned that BL had entered into an advertising agreement with Reuters, a third party, for the placement of multiple links on the Breitbart Site to promote the Reuters site.

"Indeed, Andrew was negotiating the agreement to place Reuters Advertising at the time he was negotiating the Advertising Agreement and LLC Agreement with Gen Ads."

In other words, financial arrangements for posting a story on a news site raised ethical concerns.

Journalist Greg Beato describes the arrangement as a black eye for Matt. "Drudge really used to emphasize his editorial independence. So the fact that there were these seemingly paid editorial links to Reuters.com on DrudgeReport.com looked like an ethical breach to me. Basically, it was pay-to-play."

Breitbart had expected to cash in on the deal, but instead, he told friends the legal battle put him $300,000 in debt.

While Breitbart may have struggled to pull himself out of debt, he had become adept at milking the Drudge Report for its political currency. Conservative talk show host John Ziegler recalls, "The Drudge Report was almost like the mafia and would often be used as a henchman for the conservative side . . . there were absolute quid pro quos."

Breitbart would use the power of the Drudge Report as leverage when there was a story he wanted in the mainstream news media. According to Ziegler, "He would send a link to [Mike] Allen of Politico. There would be a wink-wink, nod-nod, and voilà!: Allen posts a story. Breitbart would put the link on Drudge. It's a win-win because Allen gets the traffic and the story Breitbart wanted to circulate had been cleansed of the right-wing stench and through Politico and could now get circulated through the mainstream news media."

In another instance, Ziegler says he used the threat of a Drudge Report link after the NBC show *Today* threatened to reschedule an upcoming interview Ziegler planned to use to promote his next project. Ziegler says he called Breitbart and said, "If they bail on me, would you be able to post a story on Drudge?" After Breitbart agreed, Ziegler called NBC.

"We did the interview as scheduled. That was the power of Drudge."

In 2007 Breitbart partnered with former television correspondent Scott Baker to create Breitbart.tv, a video blog connected to Breitbart.com.

Baker first came on to Breitbart's radar while working as a local television correspondent during the 2004 Democratic Convention in Boston and his cameraman caught John Kerry's wife, Teresa Heinz, telling a reporter to "shove it." After the footage began circulating on local affiliates, Baker's phone rang. The voice on the other end said, "This is Andrew Breitbart for the Drudge Report."

Baker agreed to feed him some of the information he had on the story. Baker's footage was posted on the Drudge Report. "It was classic Drudge," says Baker. "It started with developing dot, dot, dot on the upper left-hand corner. Then came the siren. The story went up at 11:00 p.m. and everything just went crazy. Between midnight and 1:00 a.m. it had 100,000 views."

Four months later, Baker and Breitbart teamed up again after Baker learned through a friend who worked at CBS that Dan Rather was about to make an in-house announcement to his coworkers. At the time, Rather was caught up in the fraudulent airing of doctored papers that tarnished President Bush's military service, and there was a suspicion that Rather would be announcing his retirement. The speech would be fed from CBS cameras into an in-house video feed. Baker's friend agreed to put the phone up to the speaker so Baker could listen.

Baker messaged Breitbart, who was at his in-laws' house in Venice Beach. "I told him that I was going to try to live-transcribe it through IM. I begin hearing Dan talk to his staff in New York City through my phone in Pittsburgh. Then I'm typing each word as I hear it to Breitbart, who is copying and pasting each sentence, and then putting it all up on the Drudge for millions and millions of people across the world." After they had finished live-streaming the text of Rather's speech on the Drudge Report, Breitbart messaged Baker: "This is an epic internet moment."

A friendship developed, and Baker assisted Breitbart on the business side of Breitbart.com before launching Breitbart.tv in the spring of 2007. However, they faced a predictable obstacle: Breitbart owned the wire services in his own name but was still nearly 100 percent dependent on the Drudge Report for links. If Breitbart.tv was going to be successful, they would need Matt's referral traffic, and Matt was reluctant to post video. And since Breitbart still had no contract, that meant that any traffic that did come from the Drudge Report could change on Matt's whims.

"Matt would never sign anything. He didn't want to be beholden to anyone," comments a friend close to Breitbart. "Andrew was frustrated. He wanted to be his own entity."

23

HOPE AND CHANGE

During the 2008 campaign season Andrew Breitbart's frustration turned to anger after the man who hoped to become a conservative power player became convinced that Matt Drudge was using the Drudge Report as a vehicle to propel Barack Obama's campaign to electoral victory.

"The Obama phenomenon starts to happen and Andrew is on fire trying to figure out a way to derail this guy [Obama]," claims John Ziegler. "And every time he logs on, he sees Matt tipping the scales in Obama's favor."

The first sign that something was wrong came before the Wisconsin primary when on February 18, 2008, Michelle Obama remarked, "For the first time in my adult life, I am really proud of my country because it feels like hope is finally making a comeback."

At 5:39 a.m., eastern time, Breitbart put up a banner headline of a picture of an angry-looking Michelle, linking to the video under the pared-down title "For the First Time in My Adult Lifetime, I Am Really Proud of My Country." Less than two hours later, Matt took down the banner, leaving the space blank, before, six minutes later, replacing it with an article critical of Hillary Clinton, titled "CLINTON TEAM ACCUSES OBAMA OF PLAGIARISM."

According to Ziegler, Breitbart was in complete shock and simply confused. *Why was Matt refusing to go after Obama?*

In another example, after audio was obtained of Barack Obama's former preacher Reverend Jeremiah Wright making a series of inflammatory comments, Breitbart smelled blood. He posted a banner story on the Drudge Report. Once again, Matt took down the link.

Breitbart didn't give up. He continued trying everything he could to get the Reverend Wright narrative into the mainstream, including posting links to stories on the Drudge Report that had nothing to do with Obama but that would take readers to a website where a negative story on Reverend Wright would appear on a side panel. Other times, Matt would block Breitbart's access to the site entirely.

The impact of Matt tempering his libertarian instincts had a larger ripple effect on the electorate. In Ziegler's assessment, "It would have started with Drudge, then gone to Fox News and circulated throughout the rest of the right-leaning echo chamber. But without Drudge providing the fuel, the car ran out of gas. So when they are looking at Drudge and saying to themselves, 'Look even Matt Drudge isn't giving this story any credibility,' it became a lot easier to move on."

Breitbart firmly believed that if Matt had been all-hands-on-deck against Obama early on, Hillary would have become the nominee, according to Ziegler. Breitbart was angry but would only push so far, knowing that he couldn't do anything to get on Matt's bad side or risk losing the Drudge Report links that fueled his own site.

"Breitbart was just beginning to come out on his own, and without Drudge, Breitbart was toast. I told him he should quit, but he

knew that Drudge had him by the balls and that it just wasn't real-
istic," says Ziegler. "He speculated that maybe Drudge had spent so
much time in Europe he had become Europeanized."

However, according to Ziegler, Matt never hid his true motivation.
"Obama was box office. He made a business decision that an Obama
presidency would be good for the bottom line, and as it happened,
once again, Matt Drudge couldn't have been more right. It is hard to
imagine someone profiting more off Obama's election than Matt."

Before the election, when a friend was IMing his fears of what
an Obama presidency would mean for the country, Matt responded,
"Yeah, it might be shitty for the country, but it sure is going to be good
for the website."

———

Tracy Sefl was waiting to meet Matt Drudge on June 7, 2008, at the
National Building Museum in DC, where in a few moments Hillary
Clinton was going to deliver her concession speech. The end of Clinton's campaign for president marked a significant milestone for Matt.
In some ways, their two careers had mirrored each other, having
both reached new heights in popularity through the scandals that
plagued President Bill Clinton. "I need Hillary," Matt had once said on
his radio show. "That's my bank."

But at the age of sixty-one, and with a Democratic nominee heavily favored to win the White House, it marked the likely end of her
political career. Matt had reached out to Sefl, and the two decided to
attend the speech together. Sefl says, "Matt knew what side his bread
was buttered on. The Drudge Report existed in the way we now know
it because of Hillary. It wasn't so much an obsession but the foundation of who he was. As crazy as it is, they essentially made him. He
recognized that, which is why he took such an interest in her race."

Matt and Sefl tried to hang out in a back area and out of view
from the crowd, but within minutes they were spotted. As soon as
word began rippling through the halls that Matt Drudge was in the

building, Sefl's phone started blowing up. The media swarm wanted to know: Was it true? Was Matt Drudge *really* there? With her? Could she facilitate an introduction? Sefl ignored the calls.

It was an unforgettable moment. Standing with Matt watching Clinton concede, she had been struck by the feel of finality. "The world was changing, and it was changing in a different direction," observes Sefl. "When Hillary conceded, it marked the end of an era . . . Twitter was beginning. There was change in the air." It also marked a change in their relationship. Soon after, Matt and Sefl fell out of touch.

———

Matt found himself on the receiving end of an unwanted acknowledgment when in April 2009 he landed on *Out* magazine's Power 50 list. The accompanying blurb read, "What started as an email newsletter of gossip and opinion for friends in Los Angeles in the early '90s remains an essential news aggregator for political gossip junkies— of course, with Drudge's conservative viewpoints at the forefront. The internet media kingpin now runs his site from his two Miami homes—maybe he'll start stepping into the spotlight more?"

Matt was quick to refute the claim. "False. False. False," he wrote in an email to *New York* magazine. "I do not love sex with men. My site is not anti-gay. I present both sides of the anti-choice-life issue. I am not anti-tolerant! Except against big-government freaks. I liked Chaka in the eighties, and have not watched *Young and the Restless* in twenty years! But I do watch *Judge Judy*!"

It was a rare public comment from Matt. Years had passed since his last public appearance. Journalists began asking, "Where is the Most Influential Voice in America?"

In an April 29, 2009, article in the *New Republic*, journalist Gabriel Sherman wrote, "One of the most powerful figures in journalism . . . has gone almost completely underground." For the past few years, he had nearly "disappeared," supposedly because he was "bothered by the media's prurient interest in his personal life."

Meanwhile, the Drudge Report's domination over the news cycle continued to grow. "A BILLION THANKS FOR MAKING JUNE 2009— TOP JUNE IN DRUDGE REPORT'S 14 YEAR HISTORY!? PAGE HIT 675,406,735 VIEWS FROM 129,922,878 VISITS . . . TRAFFIC ROSE 21% FOR MONTH OVER YEAR AGO" blared the June 1, 2009, head-line on the right of the home page.

With Matt's popularity reaching new heights, the popular gossip-fueled website Gawker's John Cook speculated on Matt's vanishing act, writing, "Matt Drudge has always been a notorious recluse. He may be even more withdrawn from the public lately, but our source blames it on post-election burnout and exhaustion."

Behind the scenes, even once-close friends were asking the same questions. In one instance, a friend raised his cellphone and Matt raised his hands over his face. "No pictures," he insisted. "I haven't been photographed in ten years." When Matt did talk to people, he would often launch into a rant about one of his favorite topics, "psy-chic vampires," saying, "If you gave them an inch you couldn't get rid of them."

24

DRUDGE'S BITCH

Andrew Breitbart emerged from his experience covering the 2008 presidential election more determined than ever to make a name for himself. Beginning in January 2009, Breitbart launched three websites: Big Hollywood, Big Government, and Big Journalism—each a conservative critique of their respective industries.

Inspired by *The Corner*, a conservative blog on the *National Review* site, Breitbart had visions of making the Breitbart.com page a home for the right wing that would be half links and half group blogs.

"Andrew wanted the new Breitbart to be cheeky and insurgent like Nick Denton's Gawker," claims one former employee. "To create a suite of sites around hot topic areas. Hire a guy where half his salary would be dependent on traffic so you could set up your future if you did well enough." More important, Breitbart was also looking to create a stream of revenue entirely independent from Matt and the Drudge Report.

For his first story, Breitbart needed to make a splash. James O'Keefe, a young conservative activist, came to him with footage of a sting on the Association of Community Organizations for Reform Now (ACORN), a nonprofit organization that had been involved in voter registration. Breitbart seized on the opportunity.

In July and August 2009 O'Keefe and his colleague Hannah Giles visited ACORN offices in Baltimore, Washington, DC, Brooklyn, San Bernardino, San Diego, Philadelphia, Los Angeles, and Miami to produce undercover video of ACORN workers offering advice on how to evade taxes and conceal child prostitution.

Breitbart saw this supposed case of government abuse as the perfect opportunity to launch his new platform. He began shopping the story, but the questionable journalistic standards involved in the "sting operation" made it difficult to find a network willing to air it. Finally, he reached out to Glenn Beck, a conservative television and radio host. "You are the only person who has the power to get this story out," he told Beck.

Beck was sold. He agreed to air the footage. On September 10, 2009, the edited videos were published on Breitbart's BigGovernment .com and then promoted nationally, along with the website, on Beck's highly rated Fox News show at 5:00 p.m. At 5:55, the Drudge Report linked to the videos. The footage went viral. It also launched Andrew Breitbart as a major player on the conservative stage.

In an October 21, 2009, article titled "ACORN Video Creates New Conservative Star," the *Washington Post* wrote, "It is Breitbart who is being heralded as the conservative movement's new Web wizard and the answer to liberal sites such as the Huffington Post and Talking Points." Talk radio host Laura Ingraham praised him as an "internet mogul," and he was invited to speak at both the Heritage Foundation think tank and a black-tie conservative dinner, where he spoke only minutes before former Vice President Richard B. Cheney.

"They're [the liberal media] able to frame the narrative and we're always on defense," Breitbart said, according to the *Washington Post.* "The Republican Party has never had a long-term strategy on fighting the narrative. The narrative should be fought on college campuses, it should be fought through the media, and it should be fought in Hollywood, and the conservative movement is AWOL on all three."

———

By January 2010 Breitbart had once again left the Drudge Report to dedicate himself full-time to his websites. A short time later, he messaged John Ziegler that he was "glad to have 100% independence now."

Publicly, he wouldn't get into specifics for the reason for his departure from the Drudge Report. "I get to be me right now and that's the best thing about this entire thing," he told Terry Moran in a July 22, 2010, interview for ABC News. "This is the beginning of the beginning."

Asked about his relationship with Matt Drudge, Breitbart clammed up. "It's the one thing I don't talk about. Matt is an international man of mystery," he said, before adding, "The last time I saw him was running into him at the correspondents' dinner in 2005. And before that. I can't even remember . . . Right place, right time, end of story, it is what it is. It's the one thing I respect. He has his space in the media. I was the underling. I will say this—boy did I get lucky to work with Matt Drudge."

Breitbart added wistfully, "I had nothing better to do than be there on day one of the internet revolution."

However, in a conversation with Chris Ruddy, a despondent Breitbart opened up about why he left the website he had helped build. "He said he had broken a lot of stories for Matt and never felt he got the full credit he deserved," recalls Ruddy.

Unbeknownst to Matt, Breitbart had been privately plotting to directly compete with his mentor. He had been thinking about an idea to create a home page that could not only gather views independent of Matt but would also confront the conservative kingpin head-on. "Matt will never allow another home page to be created in a conservative space that could actually compete with Drudge," Breitbart would tell friends. "Never."

25

CURL

n the spring of 2010 Matt Drudge reached out to the *Washington Times* reporter who over the past dozen years had consistently sent him the kind of links he considered most "Drudgeworthy"— Joseph Curl.

The two had a long history. Curl first met Matt in person in April 1998, when he was deputy national editor at the paper. Matt was walking up a street toward the Washington Hilton to attend the White House Correspondents' Association dinner, where he was a guest at the *Washington Times* table. Curl joined him for the walk, and they entered together.

"He had become a big celebrity," Curl recalls, noting that Matt had broken the Lewinsky story just a few months before the "Nerd Prom," when 2,500 reporters and their sources, along with Hollywood celebrities and all those "famous for Washington," gathered for the annual dinner. "Everyone was coming up to him. Every journalist—even the old, craggy newspapermen who felt like they owned the joint—wanted their picture taken with Matt Drudge."

Both having grown up in the Washington, DC, area (Curl in Chevy Chase, Matt in Takoma Park), they chatted about how as teenagers they would go to Little Tavern for a bag of burgers or hit Mister Henry's, a club notorious for admitting underage club goers.

After that meeting, Curl continued his relationship with "mDrudge" on AOL Instant Messager and via email. "You didn't really talk to Matt," Curl says. "Matt would open up a dialogue box on AOL Instant Messenger in the morning. That was almost exclusively how he communicated."

Curl, like many prominent reporters of the time, kept a notebook tracking the kinds of stories Matt liked. He had become adept at catering his pitches so they would be linked to on the Drudge Report. Curl took over the White House beat after George W. Bush was elected in 2000, attributing much of his success to the Drudge Report. "When I managed to get a story linked on Drudge, my editors were ecstatic. It might drive a million hits."

It was after Curl suggested a story angle about Democratic House leader Nancy Pelosi that Matt invited him to Florida. "She was on the cover of a magazine looking forty years old and insisting the photo wasn't doctored. I suggested he run the 'haggiest' picture he could find on the wires above the link," remembers Curl.

In 2010 Curl asked Drudge (whom he called "Doc" on account of his initials, M. D.) if he was attending the WHCA dinner, and Matt replied in less than five minutes: "no dc—but want to invite you down to miami, my treat, to discuss your future, and mine! let me know."

"It was a big deal. Matt Drudge didn't meet with anyone."

Matt flew Curl first class and put him up for two nights in a suite at the Ritz Carlton on Miami Beach, telling him the stay "will be a nice break from harsh reality." The first day, Matt told Curl, "No plans for rest of day. Enjoy, sleep, rest, swim, and we'll have plenty of time to talk."

The next day, the pair met at the suite. "He was wearing shorts and a T-shirt, plus a baseball cap. I hardly recognized him without his trademark fedora," Curl jokes. They talked for four hours. He then asked Curl if he would be interested in working together on the website. Matt wanted someone to run the Drudge Report in the morning from 6:00 or 7:00 a.m. until noon every day, plus maybe a few hours on Saturday or Sunday. The deal would make Curl Matt's first full-time salaried employee.

For Curl, who had been intrigued by the power of the Drudge Report for over a decade, the offer was too good to refuse. He accepted the job. Matt bought Curl a new top-of-the-line Sony laptop and set it up with the FTP of the Drudge Report. "Guard this with your life," he said. He then gave Curl a quick tutorial on how to operate the site from his Florida condo.

To run the Drudge Report, Matt said, you had to be on top of everything that was happening in the world. "You are literally plugging into the Matrix," Curl observes. Matt told Curl the job "was like a suicide mission."

A shift working on the Drudge Report was all consuming, with Curl simultaneously scouring headlines on the internet and reading—or skimming, at least—some five hundred or more emails an hour that came through the website's tip box.

Matt told Curl, "I read something for five seconds. If it doesn't grab me, I move on."

Curl was inundated with links from friends and colleagues asking to be linked, all hoping for the inevitable web traffic sure to follow. "I would tell people, send me headline and a link, that's all I've got time to read. A hundred people would be sending me links directly. I would never play favorites. It was either Drudgeworthy or it wasn't. I never posted a single story that wasn't worthy."

The logistics of operating the Drudge Report were remarkably unsophisticated. "It is the simplest source code. It is literally 1998 code," says Curl.

The most important part came in finding the perfect Drudge link. Since Curl already had more than a decade of experience sending Matt what he thought were Drudgeworthy stories, that part came easy. Matt loved stories about weather, robots, government over-reach, and especially poking at the establishment, whether that be in Hollywood or Washington, DC. And most important, the story had to pack a punch.

Once, when Curl reached out for guidance, Matt told him to trust his own instincts. "You know the stories on the page," Matt told him. "You kept sending them to me. Just start posting them on the page." The Drudge Report, Matt told Curl, is about "being an asshole in a creative way." Another piece of advice was that the headline doesn't need to explain too much—"Assume the reader knows everything."

———

The process was simple. Once a link was selected, its destination was copied. Through the FTP, Curl would access the source code of the Drudge Report, paste in the link, then type <BR>, which put a line under it. "There couldn't have been an easier process," says Curl. "A ten-year-old today could operate the Drudge Report."

Matt had set up the system so that the page would populate quickly back when the internet came through at the speed of dial-up. "The picture is not physically on the page. He would take the address to the picture then put it on the FTP. He never used the pictures. He would just link to them. It's what kept his page really small and fast to load."

A big emphasis of Matt's was the importance of staying ahead of the news cycle. When Curl began his shift in the morning, the first thing he would do after logging on was replace whatever links had been left over from his previous a.m. shift.

Each morning, Curl logged in and saw which of the links he had posted from the day before that were still on the site. He'd scrub out a lot of them, going up and down the side columns deleting links and replacing them with fresh stories. Nearly every day, unless Matt instructed otherwise, he'd post his own banner story.

Matt had a mantra: "We are creating waves, not riding them."

"If something was posted at 6:30 in the morning and then by 2 p.m. it had gone through Fox News and Rush Limbaugh and questions were being asked at the White House press briefing, then we moved the link off the page," said Curl. "We were done with it. It was time to move on."

Matt told Curl how he and Rush Limbaugh would chat ahead of Rush's nationally syndicated radio show. "He would sometimes message Rush some thoughts right before he went live with his daily radio talk show. Then Rush would open with it. Drudge loved how he could say something to Rush, who would then repeat it to millions of listeners. Except it wasn't really coming from Rush—it was coming from Drudge," says Curl.

Matt also made clear that the Drudge Report wasn't as much about pushing a political narrative as it was about pulling in readers. In Curl's assessment, "Matt wasn't as politically motivated as most people think. He wasn't married to a political party. He was a businessman. He wanted to increase his readership and inform his readers. And, of course, he wanted to shake things up, always."

While the nuts and bolts of operating the website came easily, working for Matt Drudge also meant adapting to the unique personality that created the mystique that has for years shrouded the Drudge Report in mystery. After accepting the job, Curl was told he needed to keep a low profile, which included terminating his social media accounts. Curl promptly deleted his Twitter and Facebook profiles.

Above all else, Matt wanted to remain in the shadows. "It's like Fight Club: the first rule of Matt Drudge is you do not talk about Matt Drudge."

Two to three times a year, Matt would call Curl. When they did talk, the conversation might last three or four hours. They rarely met, but one time Matt brought him to the same hotel in Virginia outside Washington, DC, and sat him in the same booth where he said a wired-up Linda Tripp recorded Monica Lewinsky.

"I sat down, we were having a beer. And Matt says, 'Here is where it all started—right here.'"

In April 2010 Matt banned links from Breitbart.com on the Drudge Report. Matt was sensitive about people using his website to propel their own brands, and he believed Breitbart was trying to use the fame of the Drudge Report to boost his own career.

On July 19, 2010, two different video clips were posted by Breitbart to his BigGovernment.com website that, at first glance, appeared to show racism against a white farmer by Department of Agriculture worker Shirley Sherrod. The story began to lead the news cycle. But instead of linking to Breitbart's Big Government site, Matt linked to a web story that featured the video published by WCBS-TV, New York's CBS affiliate.

Sherrod would later be vindicated, but Drudge's cyber-embargo devastated Breitbart, who had purchased the wire service under the agreement that Matt would send traffic his way.

On May 28, 2011, Breitbart again led the news cycle, this time obtaining a picture from the public Twitter account of married New York congressman Anthony Weiner's erect penis concealed by boxer briefs that had been sent to a twenty-one-year-old female college student from Seattle, Washington. Instead of linking to Breitbart's site, where the story had originated, the Drudge Report linked to a *Wall Street Journal* story, sending the flood of web traffic to a rehash of Breitbart's original reporting.

Fourteen months later, the Breitbart ban was over, but the damage had been done. In becoming the brazen new face of the conservative movement, Breitbart had achieved one of his goals. But privately, Breitbart confessed he was sinking. Sherrod had launched a costly civil lawsuit against him. He hadn't received the support from Matt and the right wing that he had expected and believed he deserved. Instead, he felt he was fighting the left by himself, out on a limb, and unable to keep up with the increasing demands of his fame, all the while spiraling further into financial debt.

On July 25, 2010, Breitbart sent these messages to his friend John Ziegler:

bodiaz [11:22 A.M.]: i am in DEBT taking on the left

bodiaz [11:22 A.M.]: no institutional support

bodiaz [11:22 A.M.]: none

bodiaz [11:22 A.M.]: so my bitterness should be a mile high

bodiaz [11:23 A.M.]: i get lots of good presss, but what will that get me?!

bodiaz [11:23 A.M.]: tea party people give me high fives!

bodiaz [11:23 A.M.]: i could get laid in a geriatric center in flyover country!

bodiaz [11:24 A.M.]: and then people WANT things of me

bodiaz [11:24 A.M.]: EVERYONE

bodiaz [11:24 A.M.]: like i can wave a magic friggin wand

bodiaz [11:24 A.M.]: i fight for everything i have

bodiaz [11:24 A.M.]: and have put my family in peril

bodiaz [11:24 A.M.]: lawsuit with my house name on it

bodiaz [12:09 P.M.]: that the movement—CPAC, etc—is MOSTLY a racket.

bodiaz [12:10 P.M.]: its not one persons racket

bodiaz [12:10 P.M.]: its horowitzs restoration weekend

bodiaz [12:10 P.M.]: its a ton of them

bodiaz [12:10 P.M.]: and not all of them even see it

bodiaz [12:10 P.M.]: some are cynical

bodiaz [12:11 P.M.]: many are clueless and caught in a BAD rut bodiaz [12:11 P.M.]: and this is all they know

bodiaz [12:11 P.M.]: and are protecting their names, salaries, reps

bodiaz [12:11 P.M.]: they have NO history in selling DVDs

bodiaz [12:11 P.M.]: that i know of

bodiaz [12:11 P.M.]: why dont i do a documentary?

bodiaz [12:12 P.M.]: cause i dont think the market is there

bodiaz [12:12 P.M.]: is why im creating BH

bodiaz [12:12 P.M.]: and BG

bodiaz [12:12 P.M.]: to create a market

bodiaz [12:12 P.M.]: for a new era of conservatism

bodiaz [12:12 P.M.]: but its isnt there!

bodiaz [12:12 P.M.]: how do i know?!

bodiaz [12:12 P.M.]: im in DEBT

bodiaz [12:12 P.M.]: i owe $133k to IRS

bodiaz [12:12 P.M.]: that i DONT have

bodiaz [12:13 P.M.]: sent it in mail Thursday

bodiaz [12:13 P.M.]: and now scrambling for a loan

bodiaz [12:13 P.M.]: transfer

bodiaz [12:13 P.M.]: from dad

bodiaz [12:13 P.M.]: who is DYING

bodiaz [12:14 P.M.]: fun to ask a man at cedars getting blood transfusion and fretting about his mortality... 'heh, can i borrow off your house?'

bodiaz [12:14 P.M.]: so, LORD knows

bodiaz [12:14 P.M.]: i know that the movement sucks donkey dick

bodiaz [12:14 P.M.]: maybe i should have a breitbart cruise

bodiaz [12:14 P.M.]: breitbart conference

bodiaz [12:14 P.M.]: and become part of it

bodiaz [12:15 P.M.]: and surrender

bodiaz [12:15 P.M.]: i am sued now too

bodiaz [12:15 P.M.]: have to lawyer up

bodiaz [12:15 P.M.]: i was kidding
bodiaz [12:15 P.M.]: about cruise
bodiaz [12:15 P.M.]: i havent taken a REAL vacation
bodiaz [12:15 P.M.]: since 1993
bodiaz [12:15 P.M.]: all i do is fight
bodiaz [12:16 P.M.]: i can handle the left
bodiaz [12:16 P.M.]: not the right

———

In May 2011, Matt brought veteran journalist and *Washington Times* reporter Charles Hurt into the fold. The trio had the website humming like never before. During his five- to six-hour shifts, Curl would replace 50 to 75 percent of everything on the page with fresher and newer stories. At noon, Hurt would come and take off the rest of the old stuff. Then at 6:00 p.m., Matt took over and worked until 11:00 p.m. or later.

By the time Curl got back behind the wheel the next morning, about 25 percent of the stories he had posted were still standing. Those would be the first he would take off. Then the cycle restarted. Over the course of twenty-four hours, there would be up to 150 links flowing on and off the page.

A few weeks before the 2012 election, and just as the news cycle was heating up, Matt announced to a small group of people that he would be leaving the country. When asked where he was going, Matt wouldn't respond.

———

Matt had ended his embargo on Breitbart links, but the bad blood continued. In early 2012, after Breitbart completed the first draft of his book *Righteous Indignation*, which included an entire chapter about the near-decade period of his life he had spent working on the Drudge Report, he called Matt ahead of publication to give him a heads-up about the book and the passage about their time together.

Breitbart explained how the chapter would be an ode to the Drudge Report, with fawning praise for Matt.

"I want you to pull the chapter," Matt told him. "All of it." Breitbart said, "But this is part of my life. I spent ten years with you. I can't just pretend like it never happened."

Matt wouldn't budge—or read the chapter. Breitbart did as Matt asked and pulled the chapter. "Andrew was hurt," a friend remembers.

In February 2012 at the Conservative Political Action Conference, Curl met up with Breitbart, where the two briefly discussed the unique nature of working for Matt Drudge. "It's the weirdest job in the world," Breitbart told him. "You'll never talk to your boss—and no one will tell you what to do. It's crazy."

At CPAC, Breitbart appeared upbeat and jovial about the future, but behind the scenes pressure was building over his financial problems and perceived lack of support from the right. Later that month, video of an unhinged Breitbart screaming at Occupy Wall Street protesters began circulating on YouTube. "Behave yourself!" he could be seen shouting. "You're freaks! And animals!" Breitbart began moving closer to the large crowd, having to be held back.

"Stop raping people! Stop raping people! Stop raping people!"

"You freaks! You filthy freaks!"

"You filthy, filthy, filthy, filthy, murdering freaks."

Marc Ebner saw the footage and became worried about his friend. "I called him up to tell him I was concerned. That the man I saw shouting wasn't the Andrew I knew. We laughed about it. But I was worried he was becoming unhinged."

For Matt, the video was a step too far. He believed Breitbart was a loose cannon. "I have to do something about this guy," he said. "I've got to do something about him. I think Breitbart's getting out of hand."

———

Breitbart also realized he had to do something. On the night of February 28 Andrew Breitbart decided to stop at a local bar, the Brentwood.

He had seen the damage Matt could do by withholding links and was only a few days away from creating what he believed would be a conservative ecosystem that could support itself independent of the Drudge Report by merging Big Hollywood, Big Government, and Big Journalism, all under one site, Breitbart.com.

After arriving at the bar, he took a seat in an empty stool next to marketing executive Arthur Sando. "I knew I recognized him but didn't know from what at first, and then it hit me," recalls Sando. "He was on his BlackBerry. And I told him I had seen his work."

A debate about politics followed. Then after about two hours, Breitbart looked down at his BlackBerry and announced he was leaving. They exchanged contact information and agreed to get together to resume their debate at a later date.

Nearly an hour later, Breitbart was walking in his Brentwood neighborhood when he collapsed. He was rushed to a hospital and pronounced dead at 12:19 a.m. The cause of death was ruled congestive heart failure.

The next day, Matt posted a rare message at the top of his site.

Dear Reader,

In the first decade of the DRUDGEREPORT Andrew Breitbart was a constant source of energy, passion and commitment. We shared a love of headlines, a love of the news, an excitement about what's happening. I don't think there was a single day during that time when we did not flash each other or laugh with each other, or challenge each other. I still see him in my mind's eye in Venice Beach, the sunny day I met him. He was in his mid 20's. It was all there. He had a wonderful, loving family and we all feel great sadness for them today . . . MDRUDGE

26

FUNERAL

The day after Andrew Breitbart's death, Matt Drudge called a friend.

"I don't think I'm going to go," he said, speaking about the upcoming funeral. "I don't think I can do it."

"Matt, Andrew was your buddy," the friend responded. "It would be a huge insult."

Matt eventually decided to attend, even accepting an invitation to speak at the service. The funeral was overflowing with mourners. Among them was a small group of Breitbart staffers, including Steve Bannon. The crew had all been given specific instructions by Larry O'Connor, whom Breitbart had partnered with, not to talk to or approach Matt Drudge.

Steve Bannon, who knew of Matt's tendencies from his friendship with Breitbart, had warned O'Connor about depending on him to be a speaker. "Drudge is a recluse. He might not show."

A few minutes after the service began, Matt arrived wearing a black T-shirt, black pants, and black sunglasses. He was accompanied by Ann Coulter. "He looked absolutely ripped. It was a gun show. People barely recognized him," a guest remembers.

Matt approached Bannon. "Sorry I'm late," he said. "I don't think I can get up and talk."

"We really need you up there, Matt," answered Bannon.

"Look, I just can't do it."

Bannon told him not to worry about it. Then Matt switched his attention to Breitbart.com. The rollout of the newly revamped website was only three days away.

"So are you guys going to fold up?" he asked.

"We are moving forward full steam ahead," answered Bannon.

Matt shook his head. "The day I go, the Drudge Report is over."

He and Ann stood off to the side during the remainder of the ceremony. After the service, Matt and Coulter were invited to a celebration of life in honor of Andrew at a nearby Holiday Inn.

"I'll see you there," said Matt.

He never showed.

———

The celebration of life had the feel of a pep rally as mourners took turns lambasting the liberal establishment.

"I got a chill," remembers Breitbart friend and author Marc Ebner, who spoke at the event. "It felt like a rally. People were talking about those asshole liberals. I was like, 'Please, his grieving widow and kids are standing there.'"

Ebner says it was the first time he got the sense that Breitbart .com was going to deviate from Breitbart's vision. "Andrew Breitbart was a happy warrior. He did not have a mean bone in his body. He would not have approved of what was happening."

Within hours of Breitbart's death, a power struggle started to play out at Breitbart News over who would take charge of the website. Several staffers had urged Larry Solov to take the helm. Solov had been close friends with Breitbart, and employees thought he was best equipped to implement his friend's vision of shifting the cultural narrative.

Solov refused and instead appointed Steve Bannon as executive chairman, who at the time was best known as a conservative film-maker who helped create the pro–Sarah Palin movie *The Undefeated*. Bannon had formed a relationship with Breitbart years earlier after first lending him office space, and then working with him on the doc-umentary *Occupy Unmasked*, which portrayed the anti–Wall Street movement as a liberal plot to take down America.

The move stunned the staffers. Bannon was thought to have entrenched his position by securing a large cash donation for the debt-ridden website from the wealthy Mercer family, which had long been a major player in select conservative circles.

Breitbart.com employees voiced concern that under Bannon's stewardship the site would instead be used as his personal mouth-piece. Solov assured workers that Bannon would only be concerned with the business side and would not have any editorial influence.

In the first few months after Breitbart's death the website flour-ished, in large part because of the Drudge Report, as Matt peppered his website with links from Breitbart.

"Matt Drudge became the de facto editor at Breitbart," according to a staffer. "He was propping us up."

Like Breitbart before him, Bannon knew that depending on Matt was an unsustainable business model and immediately focused on establishing Breitbart.com as a brand independent from the Drudge Report.

"When Andrew died, two-thirds of our business came off of Drudge links. I knew we had to wean ourselves off that," says Bannon. "I made a decision very early on that we needed to be a force."

He gave standing instructions forbidding writers from appearing on Fox News, telling employees that he needed to assert Breitbart .com as a "formidable independent entity."

During the first few months of his tenure, Bannon did focus on the business end, but after about six months employees say he began to exert influence over the editorial section of the site. First, he began telling the team to do write-ups on his friends. Then he followed up by making himself a regularly bylined columnist, and then installing himself as a radio host on Breitbart Radio on Sirius XM. As Bannon became more powerful, the focus of Breitbart.com began to change.

"Bannon's involvement made Breitbart much more political. Much more incendiary. He used the site as "a blunt instrument," former Breitbart columnist Ben Shapiro observes. The website staffers, many of whom had been loyal to Breitbart, held their breath, unsure of where Bannon was guiding them.

———

On June 27, 2014, Matt Drudge was visiting DC radio station WTOP and found himself back near the small house where he had spent his youth.

Matt had emailed the previous week to say he would be in town and had inquired if he could get a tour of the newsroom. When he arrived, a station producer asked if he would like to go on the air for a few minutes, and Matt agreed. He opened the rare interview by explaining to afternoon anchors Hillary Howard and Shawn Anderson his reason for being back in the area:

> I grew up here—I grew up just up the road where 16th turns into Silver Spring, Takoma Park. The DC I'm seeing now is so vibrant. This is the center, this is the heartbeat of the nation, for good or bad. It's not going away anytime soon, and I approach it every time I get in front of a computer as "This is exciting. This is not old. This is not boring" . . . And the more people involved, the better.

Matt then opened up about the upcoming 2016 election, predicting that the defining issue would center on immigration.

"I know there are big fights throughout the country," he said. "Virginia just said, 'No, don't bring immigrants here from the border en masse.' And Speaker Pelosi is going down to the border this weekend."

When asked how he felt about an increasingly partisan press, Matt responded, "But the country is divided. All of these polls are always divided. Capitol Hill is divided. How can you say the airwaves or the website should not be divided? We are."

Matt ended with a prediction: "We're into an interesting summer here. We're only about a week into it. I'm sensing some heat. And not just from the temperature outside. I think things are heating up in many respects."

———

In late 2014 Matt Drudge approached his two employees, Joseph Curl and Charles Hurt. Matt told them that he no longer wanted them to touch the site's top stories and that they would only be allowed "to post around the edges." "I'm going to take things back."

Hurt agreed to stay. Curl decided it was time to leave.

Matt increasingly found it more difficult to trust anyone. He had always been wary that people were trying to use his name and website to elevate themselves, but after his experiences with Breitbart, where he felt used, his natural skeptical tendencies had hardened into stone. Friends he had known for decades were now viewed through a suspicious eye. Outsiders didn't have a chance.

"They are trying to make a name for themselves," Matt would tell people. "Psychic vampires. Everywhere. It's like they want a piece and no matter how much you give them, it's never enough. Never enough."

27

CAMPAIGN FOR TRUMP

A t 2:33 p.m. on July 11, 2015, Matt Drudge contacted the Donald Trump campaign to inquire about attending a Trump rally scheduled later that evening in Phoenix, Arizona.

"Thought maybe it would be fun to go. Anonymous. Offstage. But looks like may be too crazy?" he wrote in an email addressed to Sam Nunberg, who worked as a political adviser to Donald Trump's 2016 presidential campaign.

In the months that preceded the event, the campaign had been in close contact with Matt. A few minutes earlier, Trump staffers had emailed Matt a picture of a sign that read "Trump 2016—Somebody Is Doing the Raping." It was a pro-Trump sign referencing Trump's contention that rapists were crossing the border into America. Seconds later Matt posted the image on the Drudge Report. It then got picked up by media around the country.

Matt eventually made the decision to go to the rally alone and incognito.

No one in the Republican primary better understood the extent that Matt controlled the conservative echo chamber better than Donald Trump.

"Drudge first met Trump in the '90s in Mar-a-Lago. But even though Trump doesn't use email, he was well aware of the Drudge Report and would frequently check the site on his smartphone," says Nunberg.

Since its inception, the candidate had discussed how earning the favor of the mysterious man behind the Drudge Report would be critical for the campaign.

Longtime Trump friend and business associate Roger Stone credits Trump's media savvy to his years spent playing the New York City tabloids: "Historically, Trump has been adept using the media. This goes back all the way to how he played the New York City tabloids. He understands how to own a news cycle and everything that comes with it."

He elaborates, "Trump was the first politician to really understand the power of the Drudge Report and how he could use it to fight back against all the propaganda being dished out by CNN, MSNBC, *Vanity Fair*, and the Daily Beast."

Inside the campaign, showing Matt Drudge's audience that his candidacy was formidable had become a top priority. In early 2015 Trump attorney Michael Cohen helped rig the Drudge Report poll to show Trump with a sizable lead. According to reports in the *Wall Street Journal*, he did this by promising $50,000 to John Gauger, who heads the tech company RedFinch Solutions.

Matt's support of Trump would prove mutually beneficial. By July 2016 the Drudge Report had moved into second place on Similar-Web's top US media publisher rankings for the first time, just behind MSN.com with about 1.47 billion page views for the month. The site also boasted 88 percent reader loyalty, nearly twice the media average of 47 percent.

The Drudge Report also proved to have coattails. Between September 2015 and August 2016 the Drudge Report was responsible for around fifty-three million Associated Press page views, or 37 percent of that overall type of traffic for AP.org. During the same period, Matt was responsible for 22 percent of overall traffic sent to the *Hill*, according to SimilarWeb, a digital insight firm.

Matt had long known that Donald Trump translated into page views. The Drudge Report gave favorable coverage when Trump first began exploring a presidential run in 1999, and again when Matt helped fuel the "birther movement" that eventually compelled Obama to release his birth certificate in 2011 to dispel questions about his citizenship. In the beginning of Trump's 2015 quest for the presidency, it was through his son-in-law, Jared Kushner, that a connection was made.

"Jared had an instant pipeline to Drudge," remarks Nunberg. "Drudge gravitated toward Kushner because of his proximity to power. A lot of people come and go from the White House—but it's going to be hard for Trump to get rid of his son-in-law and daughter. That just wasn't going to happen, and Drudge understood that."

Inside Team Trump, there was an alternative story line being floated for the Kushner-Drudge alliance. "Inside the campaign there was a nickname for Matt Drudge—we called him Lady Drudge," says Nunberg. "Drudge had a man crush on Kushner. It was a thing." According to Nunberg, "Drudge essentially began acting as Jared's publicist. Any time anything remotely positive happened with Kushner, you would see Drudge posting a link with a flattering picture."

Regardless of Matt's motivations, no one was more appreciative of the favorable coverage than the candidate. In the morning, aides would hand Trump printed pages of different items on the internet. After seeing a good headline Trump would turn to aides, asking them with a smile, "Did you see what is on Drudge?"

28

HIDDEN IN THE SHADOWS

I n a forty-five minute interview with radio host Alex Jones, who
had become known for voicing antigovernment conspiracies, Matt
Drudge gave a rare insight into his thoughts on how the internet
had developed in 2015, the political landscape, and his own personal
well-being.

The Alex Jones Show was being recorded live on October 6, 2015,
when Matt unexpectedly walked into the studio. The controversial
radio show host appeared in disbelief at the arrival of the web publisher, who hadn't uttered a public word in over a year.

After entering, Matt stood off to the side of the set, careful to
avoid the studio lights.

"I have never had a deer-in-the-headlights experience this crazy,"
Jones began sputtering. "Because, I'm not really a fan of, like, rock
stars, movie stars, people like that. I like politics. And, I'm sitting

there during that seventy-second break, and Matt Drudge rounds the corner over here, and it was like total and complete deer in the headlights, and I'm still double-taking here. And then, he's hiding over there in the shadows right now, I'm not kidding."

Jones continued, "They're going to say this is another conspiracy theory. And . . . we got Anthony Gucciardi, is Matt Drudge over there? He is over there. Come on, just for a second to give the national media a heart attack, can you just walk over here behind the stage, or they're not gonna believe it. No, see, it's . . . Yeah, right around this way."

Matt refused to come into the light, telling Jones, "I haven't had one photo in eight years."

"What if we put a microphone into the darkness coming out of the break, and folks can do a voice print analysis to see if it's Matt Drudge?" asked Jones. "He's not gonna do it? I'm telling you, this is so classically reclusive. I wish I could do that. He is back there right now."

"It's taken a lot of work to get to this point," said Matt.

"I know it's taken a lot of work to get to this point. I admire you! Maybe I should become reclusive! Huh?" said Jones.

Jones continued, his voice rising in excitement. "We have a hot mic over there. He wants to stay, literally, in the shadows behind a curtain. But this is the king of being able to push a story out and make it the number one story in the world. They even admit that in the *New York Times* that he has more readers on politics and news than Facebook, the *New York Times*, the *Washington Post*, and *Los Angeles Times* put together . . . So he might have fifty links every day, where Facebook has five hundred million, but he has more traffic. That is the true David vs. Goliath story."

Matt's voice broke through the darkness: "Well, you were just talking about Facebook. And thanks again for having me here. Umm, I'm not on Facebook. Umm, I don't do the socials. I've got that little Twitter thing, even that's kind of disgusting. You know, I've been doing the internet as long as you've been doing this radio show, Alex, literally every day as you have literally every day, practically."

Matt continued,

I have a very clear perception what the internet is in my mind. I'm free. I'm not defined by what they say the internet is. Meaning Goldman Sachs, meaning who they invest in for the latest start-up, meaning the latest BuzzFeed, or Salon, or Gawker. Well, Gawker's more independent. But there's a lot of corporate makeover of the internet that I have not adapted to, simply put. I'm friends with some of them. When I go to New York I make the 6th Avenue rounds, but I am not a part of that system. I'm a free thinker. I'm an American. I'm *very* concerned with what's happening. So I just give it my all. I've learned how to take care of myself and detach from outcomes because, otherwise, you can't survive.

Jones replied, "I just follow my instinct because they always tell us how to adapt to be successful, but really we're just adapting to their mind-set to be their slaves."

Matt insisted, "I don't! I don't!"

"No, you don't!"

Matt continued,

I have remained *completely* independent from all of them. *All of them!* I am not influenced by *any* of them. I need no traffic from Google. I don't care if I get one traffic referral from Google, or Bing, or Yahoo, or any of these others. It's always been that way. Now, if you think of that setup, how rare that is, because everybody is so hungry for referrals, for "likes." I don't need to be liked. I don't need to be liked at all. I don't care if there's a button right there at the top of Drudge saying "like" or "dislike," "thumbs up," "thumbs down," it doesn't mean anything. Now, I hope that you come! It doesn't mean you necessarily have to like what I have up there. Now, where I've had a lot of successes, I'm getting people from both sides of the aisle. They've always said, "He's a right-wing gossip-monger," mainly because of Lewinsky and those years, which, by the way, are back. Why aren't we seeing Hillary's lovers? Excuse me. Why aren't we seeing Hillary's lovers?

Jones expressed his agreement. "That's a good question."

Matt went on, "Where is the cover-up on this? So many issues that are suppressed on a daily basis. So that's what I try to do every morning."

When asked by Jones if he was a libertarian, Matt rejected the political label. "I can't be controlled! I *cannot* be controlled! There are no interests here but what I see as the world events, *period*! That is the truth of the situation."

Of significant concern to Matt was the power of social media sites; he believed the movement was a symptom of a broader problem that struck at the heart of human nature.

He ranted that the same internet he had navigated decades earlier to successfully catapult himself to fame and fortune had now been taken over by corporations who, in their quest to monetize the flow of information, had effectively stripped it of individuality.

Matt: This whole social media stuff is bogus. Facebook, we have two billion users? This is garbage! This is designed to demoralize the individual. I'll never have two billion followers! This internet is what you make of it. It's the same now as it was in the beginning. I remember having this argument with Brit Hume once live on C-SPAN. He goes, "Oh, the internet's all UFOs and all this crap," and I said, "No, the internet is what you make of it." But in the beginning they were dismissing the internet. They were poo-pooing it!

Jones interrupted, "Isn't that good for us, that for so long they were in arrogant denial? And, they seem kind of like they're still in arrogant denial."

Matt: *No.* Now they make it over in their image! Now it's these
endless, monotonous tweets. *Meaningless! Meaningless!*
It's just a lot of gnats, a lot of confusion. When the reality
of the situation is life on earth has not changed. We need
facts, we need events, we need specifics on things, not all
this confusion. It's almost, they've made the internet over
in their image, these corporations, and I think they're failing quite . . . I think they're failing to the point, this is
a whole other discussion on how sick are the American
people right now? I've been saying they could put Hillary
Clinton's brain in a jar in the Oval Office, and she'd be
elected. People are really sick. I think you know this deep
in your soul, and this is why you get demoralized here on
this very set.

. . .

People *are sick*! How they've got here, you've been
on a wonderful arc over, almost decades now, explaining
why people are, and have become so sick. That being said,
people are willing to be made over in the image of these
corporations. The reason there's so much anger online,
also, is a newspaper like the *Washington Post* will leave
a comment section. They don't care what you're saying.
They don't care what you're thinking. That's why you
get this anger, that "Oh, I have to be," you know, "I'm out
here as a citizen, and I'm operating in their playground."
Make your own playground! The reason I'm here, Alex, is
because you've made your own playground. This is a fig-
ment of your imagination, and the Drudge Report is mine.
It is a very simple thesis: you are what you dream you are

and become. And I wish Americans would get out of the sickness and just become greater.

. . .

The internet allows you to make your own dynamic, your own universe. Why are you gravitating toward somebody else's universe? And this is kind of, again, where Drudge, to me, when I look at it right now, is a correction to this groupthink that has—there's no difference from any of these websites. You go up and down, we talk about this. What's the difference between the websites? Between a Slate or a Salon or a BuzzFeed or a HuffPo—what is the difference? There isn't any. And this is a travesty. It's almost like a weird conglomerate of groupthink that has developed in a dynamic era that should be vibrating. It should be vibrating, it should be controversial. But, I guess it's fear. Not everybody is cut from the same genetic background as you or I, Alex, of being brave, and being able to stand up. You're on the camera, I'm not. You're more brave than I am. So this is the dynamic that I'm in. I would just like to wake people up. Stop operating in their playground! Stop it!

While Matt believed he could weather "the socials," an upcoming legal challenge would ultimately strike down the Drudge Report.

Matt: I had a Supreme Court justice tell me to my face it's over for me. He said, "Matt, it's over for you. They've got the votes now to enforce copyright law, you're outta there. They're gonna make it so headlines, so you can't even use headlines." To have a Supreme Court justice say that to my face, that it's over, they've got the votes. Which means time is limited. Time is not forever. How many more moons and sunrises will you see in your life rise and fall? There's not that many! It's a small amount! So for people to be saying with this attitude, "Oh, I'll get on with my life, and my greatness, sometime." No, you can't!

. . .

So they're getting ready for these decisions to come. You thought Obamacare was shocking? You thought some of these other decisions were shocking? Wait until these copyright laws work their way up. And the Supreme Court decides you cannot have a website with news headlines, linking across the board. Then, that will end for me. Fine! . . . So I don't know why they've been successful in pushing everybody into these little ghettos of these Face-books, and these tweets, and these Instagrams. These "Instas." This is ghetto! This is ghetto! This is corporate! They're taking your energy! They're taking your energy and you're getting nothing in return! Nothing!

Jones asked about the danger in news consolidation.

Matt: There's already automated news sites. Google News, hello anybody? They actually, the idiots reading that crap think there's actually a human there. There is no human there! You are being programmed to being auto-mated even up to your news. And Apple News, I don't know what that's about. That was also creepy. A same corporate glaze over everything. I don't see the world that way. I live in a world that's free, colorful, vibrant, takes chances, bold, stands up to power, and that's where I've made my success.

. . .

I'm just warning this country that, yes, don't get into this false sense that you are an individual when you're on Facebook. *No. You're not.* You're a pawn in their scheme.

Before Matt ended the interview, Jones implored him to end his seclusion and once again put a public face to the Drudge Report.

"Maybe I'll join Facebook," Matt answered sarcastically, before adding, "No, I can't. I realize that just my personality is, that I've gotta stay focused. I can't be too distracted."

He continued,

At my height of media availability, I was doing the website, the TV show, and the radio show at the same time, as you are doing now. As you are doing now. Mine was with the corporations. The Clear Channel, News Corp., and then the Drudge Report. But, still, I felt, just myself, I felt it was just more powerful to go to the web. Plus, to not necessarily be playing in their playground. Because the power of the individual, as you represent sitting there right now, is *powerful* to the heart.

29

LIVE FEED

In January 2016 Matt Drudge began linking to live feeds of Trump rallies. By that April, the Drudge Report had become full-on weaponized in support of Donald Trump.

"We had such quick access to Drudge. If we emailed him something, it would go up on his website within minutes, nearly instantly," former Trump aide Sam Nunberg remembers.

At campaign rallies, Trump returned the favor, taking his affection for Matt public, calling him a "great guy" and often citing the results of the website's online Drudge poll that his campaign had helped rig.

As a result of the favorable headlines, Matt was given access to the Trump campaign that dwarfed that of the rest of the mainstream media. "Drudge was treated by the campaign and Kushner like he was the pope," says a former campaign official.

For Matt, Trump's nomination had also become a personal point of pride as Matt focused the vast powers of his website on methodically taking down everyone that stood in Trump's path. First, he set his sights on the morning-line favorite, former Florida governor Jeb Bush. Matt repeatedly pounded the establishment's choice with a near-daily barrage of negative headlines.

Jeb Still Refuses to Rule Out Tax Hikes.
WALKER: 'WE NEED NAME FROM FUTURE, NOT PAST' . . .
JEB STRUGGLES FROM WITHIN

Bush couldn't weather the storm and, despite raising a record sum of $150 million, on February 20, 2016, he pulled out of the race.

Next, Matt helped take down Texas senator Ted Cruz. Three days after Cruz took home the delegates in the Colorado convention, the Drudge Report linked to nine stories, each portraying the candidate in a negative light:

Savage: Cruz should disavow rigged Colorado election.
Buchanan: Apparatchiks thieve delegates for Ted
1 Million Republicans Sidelined.
Border Patrol Agents: Colorado Voters Disenfranchised.

In a radio interview, Cruz called out the Drudge Report as an arm of the Trump campaign. "In about the past month, the Drudge Report has basically become the attack site for the Trump campaign," Cruz told radio host Mike Slater. "So every day they have the latest Trump attack. They're directed at me. Most days they have a six-month-old article that is some attack on me, and it's whatever the Trump campaign is pushing that day will be the banner headline on Drudge."

Cruz continued, "By the way, they no longer cover news . . . When [we] win a state, suddenly the state doesn't matter. You know Colorado, there was no red siren on Drudge when we won all thirty-four delegates in Colorado."

Going public with criticism of Matt Drudge was an unprecedented risk in the modern GOP movement. Cruz may have been saying what the rest of the Republican field had known to be true, but by taking on the most powerful voice in conservative media his campaign was wading into uncharted territory.

―――――

Trump had another ally in the website named after Matt Drudge's onetime protégé. By January 2015 Breitbart News had fully mobilized in support of Donald Trump under the stewardship of Steve Bannon. Bannon had convinced conservative megadonor Rebekah Mercer to buy a partial stake in Breitbart News, in part by telling her he supported her preferred candidate, Ted Cruz.

A former Breitbart employee said, "Bannon was playing both sides. He was telling the Mercer family that he wasn't anti-Cruz, but just temporarily elevating Trump in a way that would help Cruz long term. But Bannon was anti-Cruz all the way."

In addition to altering the editorial direction of the website, Bannon made a series of hires that alarmed longtime staffers, including bringing on right-wing provocateur Milo Yiannopoulos, who had entrenched himself with white nationalists and the neo-Nazi movement.

Controversial attention-grabbing headlines included "Would You Rather Your Child Had Feminism or Cancer?" and "There's No Hiring Bias Against Women in Tech, They Just Suck at Interviews."

The website's embrace of the "alt-right" would have disgusted Andrew Breitbart, according to conservative columnist Ben Shapiro, who says Breitbart despised racism and used to regularly boast of helping to integrate his fraternity at Tulane University: "With Bannon embracing Trump, all that changed. Now Breitbart has become the alt-right go-to website, with Yiannopoulos pushing white ethno-nationalism as a legitimate response to political correctness, and the comment section turning into a cesspool for white suprema-cist meme-makers."

Shapiro has referred to Bannon as a "scorched-earth personal opportunist." In Shapiro's words, "Andrew built his life and his career on one mission: fight the bullies. But Andrew's life mission has been betrayed. Breitbart News, under the chairmanship of Steve Bannon, has put a stake through the heart of Andrew's legacy. Breit-bart News has become precisely the reverse of what Andrew would have wanted."

Inside Breitbart.com, employees said Bannon had become a feared figure. He would pound his fist on the desk when angry and berate employees in front of the entire newsroom who had editorial differences. It wasn't unusual for employees to be woken up with early-morning phone calls from a seething Bannon, venting his frus-trations over minor editorial details. At times, the focus of his wrath would turn to Matt Drudge. Bannon was desperate to show that Breitbart.com's survival wasn't dependent on "suckling the Drudge tit."

"I own Drudge," Bannon could be heard screaming in the news-room. "I control Drudge!"

Sources inside the Breibart.com newsroom happily relayed Ban-non's outbursts back to Matt.

30

PERFECT STORM

The zeitgeist of the 2000s saw sweeping technological improvements that thrust new opportunities onto the populace, bolstering the standard of living but also miring people in a bog of contradictions.

Despite new advancements that connected people to each other like never before in ways that would have been indistinguishable from magic just a couple of decades earlier, they were also never more alone, as the suicide rate increased 24 percent between 1999 and 2014.

Cultural norms were also evolving. Outrage over the portrayal of actor Dennis Franz's bare cheeks in the early '90s cop drama *NYPD Blue* gave way as Americans watched celebrity meltdowns in record numbers on reality TV; a Paris Hilton sex tape ushered in a new unseemly cottage industry; and "going viral" became a permanent fixture of the public lexicon.

The '00s brought us ten thousand songs in our pockets as well as the collapse of the Twin Towers, the Iraq and Afghanistan wars, Hurricane Katrina, and the economic downturn that helped usher in a new Democratic revolution in American politics led by the first African American president, Barack Obama.

The changes in the way people consumed information were even more dramatic. By 2016 the media landscape had become nearly unrecognizable from the one Matt Drudge had jumped into two decades earlier when he first created the Drudge Report. Instead of a niche market, the internet had evolved into the main source for news gathering for the vast majority of the American public.

The proliferation of smartphones meant that information had become more freely available to more people, in more places, and at more times than at any point in history. However, instead of the revenue going back to the article's source, it was now being funneled through third parties, with 62 percent of US adults getting their news from social media sites like Twitter or Facebook, hurting the bottom line and making it increasingly difficult for consumers to differentiate credible sources from bad players.

With social media dominating the news platform, the newspaper industry struggled to remain viable. By 2016 total weekday circulation for US daily newspapers, both print and digital, fell by 8 percent, marking the twenty-eighth consecutive year of declines and its lowest point since 1945, according to a Pew Research Center analysis of data from the Alliance for Automated Media. The plunging readership had a ripple effect as staff cuts decimated newsrooms across the country.

One of the first casualties was time-intensive, long-form journalism pieces, as editors began opting instead for quick-read clickbait. The early formula succeeded in attracting more readers at a fraction of the cost, but a path to translating page views into a consistent stream of revenue continued to evade publishers.

By 2016 Rush Limbaugh, the "Godfather of Conservatism," had also gone through a transformation. Limbaugh had reached a new pinnacle, with up to six hundred affiliates on his self-styled "Excellence in Broadcasting Network" and an estimated thirteen million listeners per week. But during the 2016 campaign season, the most-listened-to talk radio host in the country went through a political transformation.

While fellow right-wing hosts Mark Levin and Glenn Beck went to war against Donald Trump over his lack of conservative credentials, Limbaugh held fire—or at times even appeared to embrace the new populist politics that embodied Trump.

Limbaugh had forged a friendship with Trump years earlier, golfing together at Mar-a-Lago, where between the links Trump would pick his brain on the Obama presidency and the political issues of the day. It was only after the nomination had been decided that Limbaugh admitted for the first time that Trump had never been a conservative, telling his audience on September 16, 2016, "Can somebody point to me the conservative on the ballot?" Limbaugh asked, "'What do you mean, Rush? Are you admitting Trump is not a conservative?' Damn right I am!" He continued, "Folks, when did I ever say that he was? Look, I don't know how to tell you this. Conservatism lost in the primary, if that's how you want to look at it. We had Cruz; we had Rubio."

Limbaugh's hedging enraged conservatives, many of whom had believed a well-timed endorsement of Cruz could have helped tip the scales in the GOP nomination.

For American voters seeking news during the 2016 election, Fox News proved to be the single most important source for information, beating out Facebook, local TV, and newspapers of any kind . . . by a huge margin, according to a Pew Research survey.

Rupert Murdoch's cable channel had blown cable news competitors CNN and MSNBC out of the water, closing out 2016 as the fifth-most-watched network in prime time in all of TV, behind only the big four broadcast networks: NBC, CBS, ABC, and FOX.

The number one network in prime time had deep roots in the Trump campaign. Fox News's influential prime-time ratings star Sean Hannity had forged a relationship with Trump all the way back in 2011, when the businessman turned reality star was being featured as a regular guest to promote his theory that President Barack Obama wasn't born in the United States. The next year, when Trump was considering throwing his hat in that year's presidential election as an independent candidate, he consulted Hannity, who advised against it and would offer private strategic advice during the campaign.

When on August 9, 2016, RealClearPolitics polling showed Democratic nominee Hillary Clinton with a seemingly insurmountable advantage of nearly eight points, Trump turned to his longtime friend, former Fox News chief Roger Ailes, to help prepare for the first presidential debate.

Trump's relationship with Ailes, who earlier that year had been forced out of the network he built after women accused him of sexual misbehavior, had spanned more than a decade, with the cable news executive even consulting with then–reality TV star Trump on the launch of Fox Business. Ailes offered the Trump campaign a wealth of experience in television and politics, which began in 1968, when he left his job working on *The Mike Douglas Show* to become a political consultant for then-candidate Richard Nixon, becoming "Nixon's executive producer for television."

One former Trump campaign senior staffer notes, "Trump always knew that his base didn't listen to John McCain or Lindsey Graham. They were listening to Fox News and Matt Drudge."

On August 17, 2016, Trump made another move to consolidate the right-wing media machine when he named Steve Bannon chief executive of his 2016 presidential bid.

The *New York Times* wrote that the Bannon-Trump alliance was "a defiant rejection of efforts by longtime Republican hands to wean him from the bombast and racially charged speech that helped propel him to the nomination but now threaten his candidacy by alienating the moderate voters who typically decide the presidency."

Bannon told a gathering of conservatives, "We don't believe there is a functional conservative party in this country, and we certainly don't think the Republican Party is that." And he added, "It's going to be an insurgent, center-right populist movement that is virulently antiestablishment, and it's going to continue to hammer this city, both the progressive left and the institutional Republican Party."

Matt Drudge had successfully navigated the 1990s and 2000s by creating his own wave. He had blazed a trail that spanned generations, fusing the glory days of print newspaper gossip from the '60s, '70s, and '80s with the modern digital age. However, the man who was being touted as the most powerful man in media was about to see his influence soar to new heights.

On September 26, 2016, Donald Trump took the stage with Hillary Clinton at Hofstra University in Hempstead, New York, for the first of three presidential debates. After the conclusion of the debate, it was the consensus from the vast majority of newspaper editorial boards around the country, the Big Three, cable news, and Trump's own staff that Hillary Clinton had scored a big win. But while Trump's staffers were licking their wounds, the candidate himself was ignoring the mainstream media, instead gauging his performance through the lens of the Drudge Report.

When Trump asked former New Jersey governor Chris Christie for his opinion on his debate performance, Christie answered, "You lost."

"What are you talking about?" Trump responded. "I'm getting 94 percent of the vote on the Drudge Report poll."

31

WHITE HOUSE

Jared Kushner and Steve Bannon were sitting together on the terrace on the fourteenth floor of Trump Tower on Tuesday, November 8, 2016, despairing over the early data.

The exit polls were rolling in and they were showing what most pundits had believed was inevitable—a Hillary Clinton landslide.

Kushner turned to Bannon. "What do you think?"

"Fuck, this can't be right," said Bannon.

Kushner paused. "Let's call Drudge."

Matt picked up the phone. After Jared voiced his concerns about the early exit polls, Matt's voice turned incredulous.

"You fucking morons," Matt answered. "Fuck the corporate media," he added. "They've been wrong on everything. They'll be wrong on this."

———

Down below in the campaign's war room, Donald Trump was surrounded by several television sets monitoring the returns when he
received a call on his cell phone. It was Fox News host Sean Hannity.
He told Trump that he had seen the exit polling and that his advisers
were "picking straws" to decide who was going to give the boss the
bad news.

Moments later, the phone rang again. This time it was Matt Drudge.

"You are going to win," he told Trump.

A former campaign official said Matt took it a step further, telling
Trump he was going to win Pennsylvania and more.

"Drudge was absolutely confident," the official added.

Later in the evening, another campaign aide lifted his phone
to show Trump the banner headline on the Drudge Report reading
POLITICAL MAP COULD BE RESHAPED.

Trump smiled. "We're about to find out how smart he really is."

Matt's headline proved prophetic. Trump lost the popular vote
but won in an electoral college landslide.

———

Matt's power had reached a new apex in the Trump administration
when he took on the role of a de facto adviser. Matt was at the White
House on "multiple occasions," including a visit in the Oval Office
during the administration's first hundred days, according to Sam
Nunberg. "When he wasn't on the physical premises, he was always
in Jared's ear."

It wasn't uncommon for staffers to see Jared walking through the
walls and yelling, "I just got off the phone with Drudge."

When Matt did see Trump face to face he had a familiar refrain,
telling the commander in chief, "Don't worry about the media," in
Nunberg's words.

"Drudge is great, by the way," Trump said to *Fox & Friends* host
Steve Doocy in a June 18, 2018, interview. "Matt Drudge is a great gen-
tleman, he really has ability to capture stories that people want to see."

Behind closed doors, the president also voiced his approval of the web publisher, telling a staff member, "He's a smart guy. Very savvy. Interesting." Another official summed up the president's curiosity: "Trump thinks Matt Drudge is a star. And Trump is a star fucker. That's why you see Kanye West and Jim Brown in the Oval."

———

Six months into the Trump administration, a power struggle emerged. Both Jared Kushner and Matt Drudge wanted Steve Bannon (now the White House chief strategist) out of the administration. The main issue between Bannon and Kushner was philosophical. According to one official, Bannon felt like after the election "Jared and Ivanka became totally different people," adding, "Bannon thought Trump's kids were political lightweights. He believed Jared was stupid. Jared kept thinking the Dems wanted to work with the White House. He never understood that the Dems' only goal was to take down the president. After the election victory they suddenly didn't have time for Steve."

More important to Bannon, he believed Kushner was working to undermine the president's campaign promises to the American people and had become wary of some of the people Kushner had pushed into the administration, including economic adviser Gary Cohn and national security adviser H. R. McMaster.

"Jared is a Democrat," the official says. "That really pissed Steve off."

———

On March 31, 2017, Matt once again reemerged from seclusion, this time as an in-studio guest on Michael Savage's radio show, *The Savage Nation*:

I'm getting a little bit nervous about the media situation. The media was near death. The media was hanging on by the short hairs. Do you know *Vanity Fair* was going under? CNN barely had a fraction . . . Trump has saved the media. Record ratings now because the opposition is consolidating, they are following every bouncing ball. People actually believe Trump is a Russian agent . . . this is the drugged ones. This is the drugged ones. How do you get them off?

Matt added,

I liked Donald the man even before he ran. I think he is one of the most fascinating Americans that have ever lived in the modern era. He is a throwback. He's old school. Part of me is his personality is not totally being used here. The charm. The guy who ran the hotel. The guy who had a number one TV show with *The Apprentice*. Charisma. Charisma is needed in this job. This isn't just getting a bill through Congress. This is also charisma. So I wish they would let him return to Donald Trump—the full Donald Trump.

Matt suggested that Trump "disappear" for a while. He should "go behind the scenes" and just go to work and not be in the "public face" every day. "Nixon wasn't in your face. Since when did the president become someone who was in your face daily? I think he should just go to work behind the scenes, but I think after Bill Clinton, you had to be in the public face every day. You had to be part of the pop culture . . . I think we would respect him if he got serious things done, and the end result, you judge the tree by the fruit."

———

By summer 2017 the bad blood between Matt Drudge and Steve Bannon had reached the boiling point. Matt had never liked Bannon or the competition he brought when he helmed Breitbart News, but after the screams that he "owned Drudge" had made their way from the Breitbart office space to Matt's in-box, whatever relationship they had was gone.

"The reality is, Matt Drudge was working behind the scenes to remove Steve Bannon," a former campaign adviser claims. "Steve knew what was happening. His theory was that Drudge was jealous."

Kushner believed Bannon was only using his proximity to the White House to advance his own future. But ultimately, it would be Bannon's own words that facilitated his downfall in the eyes of the president. Trump had long fumed over the public perception that Bannon was responsible for the president's shocking electoral victory. The February 13, 2017, *Time* cover featuring Bannon above the headline "The Great Manipulator" had further soured their relationship. By the time an interview appeared showing Bannon contradicting Trump on North Korea, Trump had had enough. On Friday, August 18, seven months into Trump's term, Bannon was fired.

Trump adviser Roger Stone says Bannon "slit his own throat when he appeared on the cover of *Time*. The one thing you cannot do with Donald Trump is attempt to take credit for his accomplishments." He adds, "Steve Bannon is an amateur, and a poorly dressed one at that. I wouldn't hire Steve Bannon to wash my car. He would fuck it up. And you can quote me on that."

After leaving office, Bannon began using Breitbart News to punch back at Kushner.

In the third week of September 2017, Breitbart News ran eight articles critical of the president's son-in-law, including the revelation that he and other senior White House staffers had used private email addresses (the very same "crime" conservatives tried to take down Hillary Clinton), along with the news that Kushner was registered to vote as a woman. Another article highlighted a *Vanity Fair* comparison of Kushner to Fredo Corleone, the mafia family scion in *The Godfather*. In its lead, the article described Kushner's "track record of mediocrity and bad business decisions."

The goal was to drive a wedge between Kushner and the president's base.

Meanwhile, Kushner used the Drudge Report to lob back. In January 2018, after it was discovered that Bannon told author Michael Wolff that Robert Mueller, who had been appointed to investigate Russian interference in the election, would "crack Don Junior like an egg on national TV," Matt leaped to the president's defense.

In a January 3 tweet, Matt wrote, "No wonder schizophrenic Steve Bannon has been walking around with a small army of bodyguards."

Matt tweeted again, twenty days later: "Time to call out Michael Wolff and his fabricated bullshit! I had dinner with the president a few weeks ago and he was in fine form. He was optimistic, engaged, on top of the world, loving the job. And already talking about his 2020 re-election run."

On January 9, 2018, Bannon took another hit when he was forced out at Breitbart News. Rebekah Mercer, whose family owned a partial stake in Breitbart News, wrote in an op-ed for the *Wall Street Journal* that the publication's former chief "took Breitbart in the wrong direction."

Matt Drudge had won, again.

———

Matt Drudge had come out victorious in helping oust Bannon and had the ear of the leader of the free world. However, despite all his success, signs of paranoia grew stronger.

In January 2016 Matt gave away the 4,600-square-foot house that he had paid $700,000 cash for in January 2013. He surrendered the property to a man with whom he had shared the same addresses since 2004 for a total of $10, according to Miami-Dade County property records. The house had been stockpiled with survivalist stuff, according to a friend.

Matt told his neighbor Kevin Tomlinson, whom he befriended in Florida, that he needed to keep moving because he "believed that he was always being watched. That people were out to get him."

Tomlinson adds, "Matt thought there were eyes everywhere."

In one instance, Matt told Tomlinson he had been chased by the Clintons. Another time he said, "They are stalking me, so I'm hiding out in Poland." He would say, "They are watching me. They know where I'm at. They are going to see the cars I'm driving and get my plates."

"I was worried about him," added Tomlinson. "I still am."

In March 2015 Matt had bought a home in Arizona, spending $1.9 million in cash for a 2,939-square-foot bunker-like compound in the desert outside Phoenix. A neighbor says the house has remained so quiet, he isn't sure anyone ever moved in.

Matt would spend a month living out of a cabana at the MGM in Vegas. Next, he would travel to Tel Aviv or Helsinki for two weeks. Then he'd spend a week in Washington, DC, followed by a month in Australia.

No matter what part of the globe he was inhabiting, Matt always keeps his time on eastern standard to stay wired to the media capital of the world.

32

SILENCE

Matt Drudge had made it. His advice was sought by the leader of the free world. His creation, the Drudge Report, was worth at a minimum, hundreds of millions of dollars. The combination of influence and wealth has made Matt Drudge one of the most successful publishers of the modern era.

He upgraded his black Fujitsu laptop for a Sony VAIO laptop. He traded in his dented Geo for a black Corvette convertible. He was traveling the globe and owned several large estates. Matt Drudge seemed to have everything.

———

The Northwood High School class of 1984 thirty-year reunion gathered around a table to celebrate one of their own. Matt's self-titled book, *Drudge Manifesto*, had been propped up along with his yearbook picture. A few classmates spoke about their experiences together, and when the speeches were over, they applauded his success before the question was asked: "Has anyone kept in touch with Matt?"

Silence followed.

Matt had reconciled with his father, who he has said is suffering from neurological health issues, and bought him a million-dollar condo in Ocean City, Maryland. He occasionally visits conservative radio host Michael Savage and former Reagan speechwriter Peggy Noonan. He stays in touch with Rush Limbaugh through messaging.

Like the links on his webpage, many of those who have occupied space in Matt Drudge's past experience a brief fleeting moment, and are then gone.

Craig Seymour, his former New York City roommate, says he hasn't spoken to Matt in over twenty years. "It's sad. I would have liked to stay in touch. We were tight. I think about Matt a lot and hope he is doing well."

Jeffrey Wells, who was working as a columnist for *People* magazine when he first met Matt, says his relationship with Matt ended in 1998. "I ignored Matt's conservative politics, but began getting irritated by his Clinton coverage. He just went on and on about it. It was too much. Finally, I remember saying something abrasive to him about it and then that was it. He stopped talking to me."

But despite the rocky ending, Wells remains grateful that Matt was part of his life. "Not only did he inspire me, but it all began because of him. He always had me as a link. He's always kept me as a link, and especially in the beginning, that was a tremendous help."

Julia Phillips, who had coauthored Matt's book, *Drudge Manifesto*, tragically passed on January 1, 2002.

Former conservative attack dog David Brock and Matt haven't spoken since Brock converted to the political left.

Conservative pundit Laura Ingraham reached out to Matt after she started the website LifeZette. She couldn't understand why her old friend wouldn't link to her site. She sent several messages. Matt never responded.

Ann Coulter had a falling out with Matt. On April 21, 2017, Coulter took to Twitter to mock Matt for "promoting fake news" by reporting that the University of California at Berkeley reversed its decision to cancel an upcoming speech, posting, "Now @DRUDGE promoting FAKE NEWS: 'Berkeley reverses decision to cancel speech by Coulter' . . . Idea: Read past the headline on a press release!"

"The falling out was about populism and nationalism," a friend of Coulter claims. "They haven't talked in a long time." It is unclear if they have since reconciled.

David Horowitz says Matt cut him off after he had used his name in a fundraising letter to try to raise money for his legal costs. "He got mad at me. I ran a couple of fundraising campaigns. I may have done two mailings. Drudge didn't realize what the cost was. I think he thought I was taking money but the truth is we spent a hell of a lot more on his defense than we took in."

"I wish I could talk to him. It hurt my feelings," Horowitz adds.

Despite the dust-up, Horowitz believes the lasting legacy of Matt Drudge will ultimately be how he single-handedly broke up the long-standing liberal stranglehold on information. "Even though it ended like it did, I'm not sorry I did it. Drudge is so important. He serves a tremendous service. The papers in the country are all leftist. The media is all leftist. That will be the incredible legacy of the Drudge revolution. How he gave the little guy a chance to fight back."

Book agent Lucianne Goldberg stopped talking to Matt after a dust-up with a source.

Linda Tripp, whom Matt dedicated his book to, says the two never met.

Author Marc Ebner hasn't communicated with Matt in more than a decade. "I think the extent of our communication since 2006 and the death of AOL was he liked one of my tweets. That was it."

Kevin Tomlinson, who had met Matt while in Florida, says Matt hasn't spoken to him since he left Florida. "The last time we spoke I said, Matt, give me your new number. He said, no, just hit me up on IM. It was weird. We were friends."

Columnist Lloyd Grove says he hasn't talked to Matt since 2007 but has fond memories of their relationship. "The one thing that makes Matt stand out is that he is not animated by ideology. He is intensely curious about the world. He really wants to promote and expose things that are new or that he hasn't heard before."

Tim Griffin, who became friends with Matt while heading the RNC's opposition research department, hasn't talked to Matt in over a decade.

Tracy Sefl, who had become close to Matt while she was working on Hillary Clinton's 2008 campaign, no longer speaks to Matt, saying, "We just went in different directions."

Joseph Curl and Charles Hurt, who both worked closely with Matt for years, found their links removed from the Drudge Report without explanation.

In November 2018 Matt's mother, Claire Star, was transferred to a nursing home in Rockville, Maryland.

One by one Matt has discarded nearly everyone in his life.

33

THE DRUDGE EFFECT

att Drudge from Takoma Park, Maryland, had seemingly done the impossible. The young child from a broken family, raised by a single mom afflicted with mental illness, disowned by his father, a high school outcast who finished 341st out of 355 students, had emerged through it all to become one of the most powerful men in America.

California State University associate professor Kevin Wallsten, who served as the former president of the American Political Science Association's Section on Information Technology and Politics, studied the Drudge Report to measure the site's power and influence. "You can't tell the story of the history of the internet without telling the story of Matt Drudge," says Wallsten. "Here is this bizarre recluse with an aesthetically unpleasing website who has this massive effect on how we consume information, and no one knows anything about him or his website."

Wallsten wanted to dig deeper and reached out to a data scientist who had recorded each Drudge Report link over the course of several years and who agreed to share his information for the study. Wallsten then went to work charting the ripple effects caused by a Drudge Report link by breaking it down into separate categories, including entertainment and politics, to find out how certain types of stories posted on the site affected the media cycle.

He found that if the Drudge Report linked to a story that other news organizations were already writing about, like unemployment numbers or a new poll, the link didn't generate much of a splash. However, when the website linked to a controversial issue, it would have the power to change the trajectory of the news cycle.

Inside the conservative echo chamber, the Drudge Report's influence was even more impressive than most people had realized, according to Wallsten. "Drudge is the leading indicator of when conservatives become pissed off," he said.

By bringing together different conservative factions under one umbrella, the Drudge Report has united the right by representing their long-held fear that the elites have captured the institutions and are weaponizing them for political gain, according to Wallsten.

"Drudge is the assignment editor for the rest of the conservative media. They are all connected. Mark Levin, Ann Coulter, Rush Limbaugh are all on the same mind-set. Drudge was able to coordinate everyone. If you have people like Rush, Sean, Mark, and Ann all on the same page, that is incredibly powerful," he added.

Matt Drudge's most profound impact came from setting a new precedent for what the individual was capable of in the early days of the web. "The promise of the early internet was the democratization of the discourse. Where everyone had an equal voice. Drudge epitomizes that promise. He has become the avatar, the symbol of what the internet can do," says Wallsten.

The overall impact of the Drudge Report on society may be impossible to quantify. The site marked a clear shift in how people consumed information. In using a new technology to lead a digital information revolution, in many ways Matt led America back to its roots, to the time when newspapers developed as a populist voice for the immigrant generations of the nineteenth and twentieth centuries.

Wallsten observes, "People thought the populist movement would completely usurp the traditional media. It hasn't. But what's happened is that it has extinguished the lines between the elites and non-elites."

It took a perfect storm of space, time, technology, and one man's force of will to achieve what Matt was able to accomplish. In Wallsten's view, "In any other era a man like Matt Drudge, with his background and education, would have been marginalized. But because of the age we live in, he was able to rise all the way to become one of the most powerful men in the world."

However, Matt shouldn't expect recognition from academia. Wallsten believes there is a "blind spot when it comes to Drudge. No one understands how he works in the media ecosystem. We as academics are loath to describe the influence of single individuals. We study systems and how individuals fit into a greater whole. This idea of one great man who can spark a revolution is often beyond the scope of academia."

———

There may be no greater barometer of Matt Drudge's influence then the election of Donald Trump. Roger Stone, a longtime Trump adviser, agrees that it was Matt Drudge who unlocked the doors to the populist movement that culminated in the 2016 election.

"Prior to the rise of the Drudge Report, the mainstream media had a monolithic stranglehold on news. There were no alternative platforms for divergent beliefs," says Stone. "The rise of a vibrant, robust internet changed all that. Matt Drudge was the first one to harvest the internet in a productive way. Drudge was very important to Trump getting elected. He would set the agenda."

Doug Harbrecht, who in 1998 invited Matt, over the objections of many, "into the sanctum sanctorum of American journalism," has been in awe over how the words Matt spoke from the podium decades earlier would prove prophetic in 2016:

> They had slaved over that speech, him and Ann Coulter and Breitbart. They were so pleased to be invited and they were ready. In that speech, he set the groundwork for how the alt-right could play the victim. He was very good at that.
>
> Drudge, who begat Breitbart, who begat Bannon, who begat Trump, began a deep thread of the alt-right, antigovernment libertarianism that has now spread across the country. What no one knew at the time was that din of small voices manifested in Drudge, and the revolution in social media would soon begin overtaking and disrupting all kinds of institutions, from the press, to the government, to the economy, to foreign affairs, and it is all pretty remarkable.

———

In May 2017 protesters came to Washington, DC, to stand outside the Federal Communications Commission office, with some holding up signs to "Ban Drudge."

Inside the building, the cries of protest could be heard as the Republican-led agency discussed a proposal titled "Restoring Internet Freedom"—the first step to gutting the Obama-era policy of net neutrality.

Other signs read "Ban Online Hate Media," "Information Equality Now," and "Stop the Hate, Regulate."

Much like the fairness doctrine before it, which regulated radio and television speech, the net neutrality policy also gave the government a larger role in regulating speech, this time on the internet.

Senators and members of Congress took turns at the microphone speaking about the importance of net neutrality to the public discourse.

At one point, the crowd began to chant, "Fair communication, no discrimination."

Organizers of the event claimed to have gathered over a million signatures to voice their concern. But despite the best efforts of the protesters and politicians, the rally failed. On June 11, 2018, the repeal took effect.

The divide over net neutrality, like the fairness doctrine before it, is rooted in fears from both the left and right in how new technologies can be used as tools to achieve political ends. For many conservatives and civil libertarians, net neutrality was a Trojan horse that would be used to silence right-leaning media.

The *Hill* reported that, at a 2009 event hosted by the Safe Internet Alliance, Republican senator Marsha Blackburn said, "Net neutrality, as I see it, is the fairness doctrine for the Internet." The creators "fully understand what the fairness doctrine would be when it applies to TV or radio. What they do not want is the federal government policing how they deploy their content over the internet . . . They do not want a czar of the internet to determine when they can deploy their creativity over the internet."

Donald Trump put it more bluntly in a 2014 tweet: "Net neutrality is the Fairness Doctrine. Will target conservative media."

It is the repeal of the fairness doctrine in 1987 that helped launch the explosion of new media and the deep polarization of the public that resulted. According to Princeton University historian Kevin Kruse,

> Before the fairness doctrine, most media tried to come very close to the center to get an objective point of view. When it was killed, it opened the door for a new world of media where you didn't have to present both sides. With the end of the fairness doctrine and the rise of talk radio and then

the internet, you have a very fractured media landscape in which you don't have to offer both sides. You instead press one point of view very aggressively. And so you had the rise of Rush Limbaugh, the rise of Matt Drudge, where the same pattern held true. Drudge saw an opening, and he took advantage of it. You had the creation of, then, Fox News. And there were efforts on the left to try to counter this. They were never as effective as those on the right. But you see the media landscape start to fracture, and so politics becomes incredibly polarized.

However, the partisan media that exists today isn't without precedent. Kruse notes, "If you go way back to the early days of the American republic, sources were very, very partisan. Throughout the eighteenth and nineteenth centuries, papers would literally name themselves after a political party and take the party line. What we have now is similar in partisanship but different in scope. There is now this unprecedented torrent of information."

However, the solutions being proposed, like net neutrality, which are usually top-down attempts to create a level media playing field, are unlikely to succeed, in large part because the media market is dictated by the laws of supply and demand. Any tinkering with that formula in the dissemination of information is sure to be looked at by an increasingly skeptical public as manipulation. When after the 2016 election Facebook and Twitter attempted to try to insert different perspectives into news feeds, people rebelled, forcing the tech titans to revert back.

Likewise, after Microsoft installed a controversial fake news filter called NewsGuard, which gave the Drudge Report a red warning label of "failing to maintain basic standards of accuracy and accountability," a backlash in the conservative media sphere promptly followed.

"We could push back," says Kruse, "but I don't think you can put the genie back in the bottle. It just won't fly in today's day and age."

Linda Tripp, whose tapes spurred the story that launched the digital media revolution, has had more than two decades to reconsider her role. Tripp doesn't dispute the accuracy of Matt's reporting but has questioned the motives and ultimate end goal of those from whom she had sought help.

"We were all clumped together in the right-wing conspiracy. I knew nothing at the time, but it might not be all that far off to suggest [a conspiracy]," says Tripp.

After releasing the tapes, Tripp endured death threats and an unprecedented public shaming. She moved to the country and unplugged from society, spending the next several years of her life without a television.

Tripp has no doubts that she did the right thing—that President Bill Clinton had abused his office and she had an obligation to get the information into the hands of authorities. But looking back, Tripp says she also feels used:

> Everyone had an agenda. Everyone was very politically driven. Nothing was transparent to me. I was drowning. I would have taken help from Satan at the time. The only thing I knew was that I needed to get the tapes into the public domain come hell or high water. In a way, there was a right-wing conspiracy of people working to take down the president. I guess I was part of it, except I was the last person to know.

How much longer Matt will continue helming the Drudge Report continues to be a source of speculation.

By April 2017 Charles Hurt had left the Drudge Report to become editor of the *Washington Times* and Matt had hired Daniel Halper, the former Washington bureau chief of the *New York Post*.

In the Age of Trump, the news cycle has never been as juiced. The Drudge Report's page views have continued their upward trajectory.

From December 2015 to December 2018 there have been a total of 55,136,650,898 page views of the Drudge Report, with 146,000,000 average monthly visits, according to SimilarWeb. From January 2018 to January 2019, over eleven billion visits were recorded to the Drudge Report, according to Quantcast.

However, a lifetime of being hunched over a computer for as many as seventeen hours a day has taken its toll on Matt's body. He experiences pain in his back, neck, and shoulder. His spine is curved, and he has one foot "that is turned out in a way."

"Don't try to live my life," Matt once told a friend. "It's horrible."

Drudge Report watchers say there has been a noticeable slow-down leading into 2019. The page doesn't update quite as quickly as it once did. Many can't remember the last time the Drudge Report broke a major story.

Longtime Republican consultant and Reagan biographer Craig Shirley believes social media is taking its toll on Matt's ability to crash a news cycle, saying, "Twitter now moves a story much faster than Drudge does."

"It isn't what it used to be. But [the Drudge Report] does still drive traffic," says a digital editor at a New York City newspaper. "It's just now if you get a link, it very slowly begins to pick up steam because it first has to go through social media."

Tracy Sefl believes that time has finally made the Drudge Report outdated. "I don't think his site wields the same influence. It's very different," she says. "It's not as relevant. And it's not Twitter. It also lost the characteristic whimsy that was so Matt. My theory, having known him a long time, is that he's not nearly as central as he used to be. His heyday is over."

Sefl still believes that history will one day reflect kindly on Matt Drudge and the revolution he started. "One thing I took away from Matt . . . He was writing his own rules of journalism."

When Matt is ready to log off the Drudge Report for the last time, he is unlikely to name a successor. Once when an NBA owner offered

Matt $150 million for the Drudge Report, he refused, saying, "I could just take the money and walk away and never look back, but then they are going to run the site under my name."

Just as the Drudge Report usurped the mainstream media, Matt seems resigned to his fate that one day another disrupter, whether it be social media or some yet-to-be-dreamed-of technology, will one day cast him off.

The cycle continues, always moving forward.

"One day you'll look at Matt Drudge and remember when he was so hot back at the turn of the century. I'll accept that," he said in a 2003 interview. "I'm not going to have the bitterness of the Ted Koppels of the world, who can't accept that new technology has pushed them into irrelevance."

"I've had a helluva run . . . Helluva run," he told Alex Jones in 2016. "I couldn't have gone any further . . . I feel I have gone as far out of the galaxy as I can on this. I still wanna stay out here, but I've gone pretty damn far for what one individual can do in this culture."

Andrew Breitbart once told a friend that the way Matt Drudge leaves the world of journalism will be exactly how he arrived more than two decades ago: on his own terms.

Breitbart added, "One day people will try to go to the Drudge Report and there will be nothing there. The page will be all white. No message. Nothing. Like performance art."

ACKNOWLEDGMENTS

This book is only possible because of those who graciously shared their stories with me.

Michelle Brooks, Joseph Curl, Ben Shapiro, Tracy Sefl, and the countless others who felt this moment in history was too important to be lost.

I also owe a debt of gratitude to the tireless work of my agent, Elaine Spencer of Knight Agency, who believed this was an important story that needed to be told.

I cannot say enough about the professionalism and expertise exhibited by the entire team at BenBella Books. Publisher Glenn Yeffeth and editors Joe Rhatigan, Leah Wilson, and Alexa Stevenson worked to bring this manuscript to life.

I also owe a debt of gratitude to several other people, including Casey Reiland, who helped with research.

My family was also instrumental in the completion of this book. My daughters, Isabel, Hilde, Georgia, and Juliet, kept the screaming in the house to a minimum during interviews. I am very appreciative.

To my wife, Bridget, you are the first page, the last page, and all the pages in between.

INDEX

ABOUT THE AUTHOR

Photo by Hilde Kate Lysiak

Matthew Lysiak was a staff investigative reporter for the New York *Daily News*, where for ten years he covered national stories across the country, including the death of Trayvon Martin, the BP oil spill, the shooting of representative Gabby Giffords, and hundreds of other national stories. His exclusive coverage of Occupy Wall Street and the 2012 shooting in Sandy Hook, Connecticut, brought him national attention. In 2013 he left the *Daily News* and published *Newtown* (Simon & Schuster) and *Breakthrough* (HarperCollins) and coauthored the six-book Scholastic series *Hilde Cracks the Case*. He has appeared on *NBC Today*, Chris Matthews's *Hardball*, the *Kelly File*, *New Day on CNN*, and dozens of other television and radio outlets to promote his work. The story of his family is the subject of *Home Before Dark*, a television series on Apple TV+ starring Brooklynn Prince and Jim Sturgess. Matthew lives with his wife, four daughters, and his dog in Patagonia, Arizona.